Against All Odds

Two Pennies, A Rainbow and A Woman Called Mercy

By Susan Abar

Dee Ann
In God We Trust

With joy in the Lord
Branson, MO
Romans 8:28
May every penny remind
you of God's
love for you

Against All Odds
© 2010 Susan Abar

First Printing May 2010
Second Printing July 2010

For information, please contact
www.susanabar.com or www.thecoppercoins.com

Cover Design Tim Cocklin
Flower Garden Image © Filip Fuxa
Image of Girl © Lev Dolgachov
dreamstime.com

www.worldsofwonderpublishing.com

ISBN 978-0-615-32059-5

Against All Odds

Two Pennies, A Rainbow and
A Woman Called Mercy

By Susan Abar

This is a true story about an ordinary woman, imperfect and hurting, beautiful and hidden. It's an extraordinary story because God authored it in a way that she could not. It is written to give you encouragement and hope for your life's journey.

In Memory

In memory of my father and mother
Fredrick Abar and Gwendolyn Francis Booth Abar

Dedication

This book is dedicated to cancer patients and survivors, to friends and family, and to caregivers and members of the medical community. This book was written to encourage you and plant seeds of hope.

Acknowledgements

Many people have been part of this book. Some of you knew me as a child or a teenager, others of you knew me as a college student or teacher. Some of you knew the business woman, while others knew me as a struggling mother. All of you knew a bit of me, but not all of me. Each one of you has touched my life. You know who you are and the part you have played in my life's story and this book. Today, I celebrate you, the men and women in my life who are not named in this book as well as the men and women who are.

I celebrate my children, Kirsty, Aubrey and Bridget. You are precious, beautiful and loved beyond measure. You know my flaws and my failings and still, you love me. You were there through the difficult times and the good times. Know that my love for you will go on long after I am gone. To my son-in-law and daughter-in-law, Warren and Angie, you are both treasures, and I am blessed that you are part of my family and that you have invited me to be part of yours. To my sister and brother, Lynne Coulter and Fred Abar and their families, I love you.

To Ron Berger, Barb Webster, Marsha Sparks, and Tim Cocklin, you are amazing! You gave of yourselves so that others might read the story of God's miracle. You know better than anyone that this book would never have been written without you. Thank you.

To my friends, Harriet Sandefur, Tina Clark, Nance Lindstrom, and Barb Olson, you were there through it all. No one could ask for more in a friendship. You gave your love and carried my burden and made my difficult journey easier.

To Custer Road United Methodist Church, to Tom and the pastoral care ministry, and the women and their husbands of The Welcome Class: Judy and Renee Aredts, Lori and Jeff Carpenter, Sandy and John Carris, Tina Clark, Annie and Walter Dean, Mary and Doug Darin, Lori and Frank Engels, Nancy Evans, Sarah and Drew Kindseth, Lynne and Randy Laminack, Kim and Paul Hagerty, Ron and Felicity Johnson, Kathy and Mark Kingsolver, Nance and Rich Lindstrom, Barb and Bob Lovelady, Carmen and Scott Moran, Debbie and Tommy Mrazek, Barb and Randy Olson, Sheryl and Jerry Sodorff, Lynda Starnes, and Becky and Alan Wilson, you were the hands and feet of Christ. You fed me, nursed me, cared for me and lifted me up. Remembering Janine Wilson, who lost her battle with lung cancer in 2009, I want her family to know that Janine was my patient advocate and went with me to my first doctor appointment to support me. She helped me laugh when I least wanted to laugh. Janine was very special to many; I wish she was here to see this book completed.

To GNO, you know who you are Judy Dixon, Chris Jennings, Chris Koth, Esther Hopkins, Joan Owens, and Sue Gerstle. I cherish our friendship. To Amelia's Women, the first graduates of Power of Self, you are still influencing my life after all these years. To my bosom buddies, my breast cancer support group, Shelley Van Derven, Jenise Bobo, Wendy White, Yvonne Halvachs, Jenny Birge, Lori Strohla, and Sarah Pheil, as we celebrate survivorship, we mourn Melissa Ricks's passing. She was too young too die; her death came far too soon. To the women at Curves, especially Linda Mitchell, I thank you for your encouragement and smiles; you keep me focused on taking care of myself so that I can give to others. To family friends and neighbors, Cindy Cocklin, Jennifer Sugitan, Shanna Mayfield, Michelle Whitaker, Karen and Scott Ripple, Trudy, Jay and Ross and Cale Gillum, Eileen and Tony Alleman, Carol and Jim McGuire, and Linda Cubero, I thank you for all you have done and continue to do. To my friends who have never lost touch, Mona Ashley, Terri Genshock and Sherry Batts, your friendship has been a blessing. And to Larry, little did either of us know that God would use you the way he did. I am grateful for your kindness.

A special thank you to long time friends who have known me forever, Carolyn Bruton, Gloria "Gem" Campbell, Linda Gibson, and Lee Turner. And to my college roommates, Carol Carpenter, Ruthie Flemming and Karen Priest Barret, may no one ever have to eat chocolate chips in red Jello or face a Siamese cat on the stair case. Please pass the lemonade... and while I'm at it, please pass the sugar too.

To my friends at Coffee House and Stonebriar Community Church, Mary Dean, Les Fleetwood, Karen Hawkins, Derrick Jeter, Angela Paxton, Andrew Scriven, and Esperanza Pastore, I thank you for your service and leadership. To Roberta Bower, you are an amazing woman. I treasure your words, your faith and the depth of your commitment to our God. And to the women of Butler Pennsylvania, I will never forget you. You are diamonds in the sun. Thank you, Jennifer, Sue and Gigi for polishing my diamond.

To my childhood friend, Winnie Hamilton, PhD and members of the medical community, who, like my doctors Dr. Hampe, Dr. Stokoe, Dr. Kruger, and Dr. Abbruzzese are dedicated to saving lives and finding cures, your job as messenger and healer is not easy. Thank you for staying the course. To the men and women who are in the trenches and behind the scenes doing blood work, filing insurance papers and yes, even cleaning floors, you are not forgotten, and I honor you and thank you for everything that you do. And to a woman called Mercy, Mercedes Phillips, your prayers to be a blessing were answered. God uses us when we least expect and in ways we may never comprehend.

To God above, I praise you and glorify you. Thank you for your miracle, a second chance and the opportunity to be your witness and share your amazing story when the odds were stacked against me. Thank you for multicolored rainbows, your mercy and two small pennies, those seemingly insignificant copper coins imprinted with the most significant four words a people could ever build their lives upon—In God We Trust.

Contents

Introduction

I completed the book on March 4, 2010 and sent it to my publisher. That evening, I received a call from my nephew Jim, telling me that his wife Michelle, the mother of their two boys, James and Nathan, had just passed away from lung cancer. Michelle was 35 years old. She died the day before her 36th birthday.

I do not know why one person dies and another person lives to tell the story of healing—the awesome story of a miracle. I have learned that it is not my place to question God or ask, "Why?" My life's purpose is to tell this story so that you might be encouraged in your walk in faith and experience hope and a future in the gift of God's mercy and grace—even in the midst of life's most difficult circumstances.

Two roads diverged in a yellow wood,
And sorry I could not travel both
And be one traveler, long I stood
And looked down one as far as I could
To where it bent in the undergrowth ...

Robert Frost (1874–1963)

1

Crossroads

Crossroads

Redmond, Washington
Saturday, August 30, 2003

The golden rays of the early morning sun warmed the crisp morning air and wakened me gently. I turned on my side thankful to lay quietly with no need to get up and no reason to hurry.

The events over the course of the previous three months had left me exhausted and numb. Each one had come on the heels of the other, each event more devastating than the one before—each so unexpected: the layoff, the breast cancer and then the discovery of a mass on my pancreas.

In my hotel room with only my thoughts for company, I questioned my sanity for accepting the invitation to fly to Redmond, Washington, 1,800 miles from my home near Dallas, Texas to interview for a job that I, in my current condition, had no business accepting. I lay there considering what had caused me to refuse to give up my own agenda and go on living my life as if I had control over the future or my own destiny. And I wondered what had motivated me to go forward with my life as if I didn't know that my mother, like her father thirty years before her, had died in seven short weeks after being diagnosed with pancreatic cancer.

Trying to make it all go away, I laid there wondering if it was possible that my doctors had made a mistake or that somehow my scans had been misread or mixed-up with another patient's scans. But the brutal truth kept returning; there was no mistake. There was no misinterpretation or mix-up. I had had two sets of scans on two different days. The scans didn't lie—the mass was there. And according to the radiologist's report, the mass was growing rapidly.

Determined to leave no stone unturned and explore every option available to me, an appointment was arranged for me to get another opinion with an oncologist who specialized in pancreatic cancer at MD Anderson Cancer Center in Houston, Texas. A five hour drive from my home, the appointment had been scheduled for Tuesday, September 3, 2003, only three days away.

Before flying to Redmond, friends had given me the name of a lawyer, a friend of theirs, who upon learning about my situation made room in his schedule to help me get my papers in order. In less than 24 hours, my will and all the legal documents pertinent to my illness and impending death were completed and signed. Because my children were grown adults who lived in states far away from Texas, I decided to leave copies of my will and other papers my children would need and want in my filing cabinet where they would be able to find them easily. As for the original will and other important documents, I decided to give them to my close friend, Harriet. Harriet had agreed to act as my power of attorney and manage my affairs in my children's absence.

Harriet and I had been friends for over twenty years. In good times and bad she had been there for me as I had been there for her. Our friendship had not just weathered kids, divorce and second marriages, our friendship had grown because of them. Over the years, when we were overwhelmed with life's challenges and responsibilities as single parents, we listened and encouraged one another. Harriet and I had prayed for each other. She knew me better than anyone and had my best interests at heart. She knew my children, and I knew I could trust her to carry out my wishes and count on her to do what was right for my children long after I was gone.

When Harriet and her husband Jack learned of my cancer and my appointment with the oncologist at MD Anderson, they invited me to stay with them in their home less than an hour's drive from the medical center. I accepted. I knew that staying with them meant that I would have both the physical and emotional support I would need for doctor visits, treatment and if needed, surgery. And if the doctors at MD Anderson gave me the diagnosis I feared, I would have a comfortable place to stay among friends before going into hospice.

Working under the assumption that in all likelihood I would receive a job offer after interviews with team members in Redmond were completed, the recruiter had arranged for me to meet with their local real estate agent the day after the interviews. In an attempt to make the transition into the job in Redmond as seamless as possible if I received an offer, the recruiter had gone out of her way to remove all obstacles and scheduled my appointment with the agent for 10 o'clock that Saturday morning. I glanced at the clock on the hotel's beside table. The time registered a little after 9:00 am, and the real estate agent was scheduled to pick me up at 10:00 that morning.

Reluctantly, I willed myself to my feet and padded across the room to the bathroom. Turning on the faucet to the shower, I slipped out of my pajamas and caught a sideways glimpse of the reflection in the mirror, the reflection of a familiar, but distinctly different form. I hesitated before looking again...afraid of what I would see...afraid of what I would not see. My eyes tracked the still-healing horizontal scars that crossed my chest like two six-inch dashes marking the place where my breasts had been...breasts that once nourished my babies...breasts that once defined me as a woman.

I was the one who had decided to have the bilateral mastectomy. I had hoped that removing both breasts would reduce the risk of the breast cancer spreading. Never once did I consider that a far more treacherous foe might be lying in wait, hidden deep inside my abdomen.

Steam from the shower enveloped the room like a heavy fog and the breastless image in the mirror faded. I stepped into the shower acutely aware that in all likelihood, I would not live to dance at my son's wedding only nine months away. The warm water that cascaded over my shoulders calmed me, but did not erase the knowledge that I would never see my youngest daughter pick out her wedding dress or see the joy of motherhood in my eldest daughter's eyes when she held her first-born child in her arms.

Unable to hold back my tears, I wept for the chapters in the book of life that I would never live. I cried until all my tears were spent and washed away.

Turning off the water, I dried myself off and slipped on my bra. Adjusting it to the left and then to the right, I stuffed each cup with a soft cotton sock, determined that neither the real estate agent nor the rest of the world would ever know of my tears or the incisions that crossed my chest.

Putting mascara on my lashes and an extra brush of blush on my cheeks, I stepped back and studied my make-up with a critical eye and concluded confidently that I had achieved my goal. No one would ever know by looking on the outside that I was dying on the inside.

Therefore, I will soon fence her in with thorns; I will wall her in so that she cannot find her way. Then she will pursue her lovers, but she will not catch them; she will seek them, but she will not find them. Then she will say, "I will go back, to my husband because I was better off then than I am now."

Hosea 2:6-7

2

Crazy Busy

Crazy Busy

Plano, Texas
Saturday, May 31, 2003

I am an achiever by nature... determined and strong willed...eager to accomplish every goal set before me. Interwoven with a love for adventure, my nature has been my blessing, and it has been my curse. It is my blessing because it has given me the ability to be persistent and resilient in the face of obstacles; it has been my curse because I don't always know when to quit or take the path of least resistance.

It has taken me a long time to understand that the walls that block one's path in life are not always obstacles that must be scaled. I have finally learned that some walls are meant to be climbed and some are not. Some walls test our strength and resolve, while other walls protect us from impending danger lurking on the other side. Some walls are meant to be walked around, and some are there to turn us around. Some walls are not walls at all, but thorny fences that cannot be scaled by any form of ingenuity or self-will. Thorny fences are not meant to be climbed; they have a different purpose...to bring us to the end of ourselves...to bring us to our knees.

All my life I have been busy, crazy busy. I can barely remember a time when I wasn't doing something. When I was a child, I was involved with school and youth group, homework or music lessons. College was just more of the same. The habits I formed when I was young followed me into adulthood and the world of work. And with the advent of motherhood and the birth of each child, each day became exponentially busier than the day before.

Lack luster feelings of self-worth drove a misguided belief that if I just did a better job at what I was doing, others would approve of me, and I would feel better about myself. That belief drove my choices and my behavior.

Spurred on by a self-imposed need to be perfect, women's liberation and the rhetoric of women who, often without children or spouses, espoused that women could do it all, I clung to the idea that if these modern-day women could have a successful career and thrive without the support of a man in their lives, then I, a single mother of three, could do the same if I just put my nose to the grindstone and worked harder. Refusing failure as an option, I bought into the marketing lingo of the "work smarter-not-harder" gurus. And I carried my two inch binder complete with a yearly calendar and daily task sheets. As technology advanced, I traded in my binder for a Blackberry in an effort to stay in the ranks of the multi-talented, multi-tasking geniuses. My efforts were not in vain, but like the laundry, the work never really completed. At the end of the day, there was always more that needed to be done.

Sitting on my patio that last Saturday in May, I realized in the stillness of the moment that this day was a first for me—a first in many ways. It was the first time in my life time that I could remember that there was nothing pressing that I had to do. I had no children to get ready or dishes to clean, no last minute shopping or appointment to rush off to, and most significantly, I had no job to go to.

Settling deeper into my chair with a warm cup of tea in the palm of my hands, the rustling and cooing of two gray doves courting on my neighbor's roof interrupted my thoughts. Surprised by their presence, I turned my head and watched as their little eyes watched me with the same curiosity that I had for them. Startled by a sudden gust of wind and leaves rustling in a nearby tree, the doves flew away leaving me with the realization that I had no knowledge that mourning doves nested anywhere in my neighborhood, let alone could be found cooing on Scott and Karen's roof barely 15 feet from my patio.

Surveying the weathered wooden fence that lined the perimeter of my yard, I realized that, except for the neatly-trimmed grass and a young maple tree that had been planted by a former owner, my yard was barren. From the day I moved into the house, I had dreamed of a little garden, complete with flowering shrubs and colorful roses. But the fact was...I had always been too busy being busy to take time to smell the roses let alone plant them. In the quiet of the moment, I was also acutely aware that from the time I moved into my little house three years before, I had never taken the time to just sit in my backyard and enjoy a cup of hot tea.

In the blink of an eye, my life had turned upside-down, and all that busyness that made me feel so important changed in a heartbeat. I winced at the thought of that day in Larry's office two weeks before when he said, "This is the hardest thing I have to do." Sitting on the patio recalling his words, I asked myself the question, "What was the hardest thing I had ever done?"

The answer came quickly. Being a single parent had been the most difficult thing I had ever tried to do. The decision to divorce the children's father and move from our home in Kingston, Jamaica to Texas had not been easy either.

The divorce had come after nine years of doing everything I could think of to make the marriage work. In truth, our marriage was headed for disaster from the day it began. In simplest terms, I wanted unconditional love... someone to love me...someone to whom I could surrender my life who would make me feel good about myself. As for my husband, he wanted to feel good about himself also, and he had learned that he could do that when he was in control. In psychological terms, I had no boundaries, and he had none either. Over time, the lack of boundaries and our inability to communicate spiraled into the classic case of a dysfunctional marriage complete with all the drama of emotional and physical abuse. Reaching a stalemate when counseling failed to resolve our marital issues, my instincts as a mother won out. I was not just a wife, I was the mother of our three small children, and their welfare was more important than anything else.

Divorce gave me two new titles: divorced mom and single parent. Neither title gave me any comfort; in fact, having grown up in a challenging, but intact family, the titles seemed to announce to the world what I wanted to acknowledge least... "failure."

The divorce freed me from the marriage and the emotional and physical abuse of an unhealthy codependent relationship, but following quickly on the heels of that freedom was the reality that being divorced had some serious drawbacks and carried new challenges.

I never expected the responsibilities I faced as a single mother to mushroom exponentially or that those same responsibilities would become challenges that would force me to mature in ways that I was not prepared for. Tasks that had once been divided between my husband and me fell solely upon my shoulders. Trying to be the breadwinner and a mother was not easy for me or for my children. As a teacher, I found myself grading papers and preparing lesson plans while my children, once accustomed to coming home from school to find their mother preparing dinner, learned the ways of latch-key kids who came home to a parentless house and started their school assignments on their own.

Being a single parent had an impact on my finances as well; it put me on the fast track to near poverty. Having one income and doing more with less didn't always work. The numbers in my checking account bore witness to the fact that feeding the children and paying the rent and utility bills every month absorbed everything I earned as a schoolteacher. Barely able to pay the monthly bills let alone save for the children's college or the future, I enrolled in night classes and earned a second degree, this time in business. I was confident that my new credentials and additional knowledge would open doors to a better paying job. It took me fifteen years of effort and working in lower paying jobs to land the job of my dreams in the corporate world, and when I did, I was more determined than ever to prove myself.

Only my children did I profess to love more than my job, but in truth, my behavior spoke quite the opposite. Working long hours didn't bother me. I prized my job and the benefits that went with it. In the corporate world I felt important, appreciated and rewarded for what I did. And I liked the feeling that came with being empowered to make decisions. I may have said that my children were the most important part of my life, but the time I spent away from them at work working, belied my words. I loved my family dearly, but being a career woman left little time for my family. In my need for affirmation and approval from others, I was determined to be self-sufficient and prove myself through my work.

Raised in the Midwest during the era of women's lib, I had learned to take pride in opening my own doors and carrying my own luggage. And over the years, I attempted to become a modern day superwoman, determined to show the world and the children's father that I, a single mother, could take care of my family and make it on my own.

Settling in Plano, a suburb of Dallas, had been a good choice. Plano was a great city to raise my children, and I loved the mild seasons and not having to deal with five months of cold weather and dressing the children in snow suits and boots everytime they went outside. My first winter in Texas proved I had made the write decision - not having to shovel snow delivered by Arctic blasts that crossed the Great Lakes and inevitably ended up blocking the driveway of my parent's house during the winter months in the state of Michigan where I had grown up was the best reason of all to stay in Texas.

Sitting on my patio looking at the perimeter of the property where the lawn met the fence, I realized that I had spent my entire life being busy...too busy to hoe the flower bed that I longed to build and too preoccupied at work to think about where I might plant a shade tree or the daffodil bulbs my youngest had given me for my birthday.

Taking one last sip of tea, I looked at the bottom of my cup; it was empty. Getting up to refill it, I thought about my children and all that they meant to me. The scent of ginger and lemon in my tea cup lingered in the recesses of my mind as I poured. Adding a little sugar, I smiled. Having children added a certain spice and sweetness to my life. Their antics that I had considered catastrophes were nothing of the sort; they were, as Kahil Gibran so aptly wrote, "... life's longing to be free." At the time, freedom for them was the furthest thing from my mind. All I wanted was for them to behave... to be perfect children.

How little I understood about life and motherhood then. I wanted my children to be perfect, so that I would look like a perfect mother in the eyes of others. My focus had not been on them as much as it had been on me. My focus had not been on guiding my children to develop their God-given talents to discover their life's purpose, but on how others measured their talents and perceived them. How wrong I was. My children were not perfect; they were perfectly normal. With time and experience under my belt, I learned that their rebelliousness as teenagers provided critical learning moments for my children that laid the foundation for how they would think and act as adults. It was during those teen-age years when my children were pushing the envelope and chomping at the bit to become their own persons that the concept of cause and effect became embedded in their psyche as they experienced the consequences of their choices and their behavior.

Those learning moments for my children were teaching moments for me, and clearly, I never earned the teacher of the year award. Parenting was pretty much trial and error and parent excellence was not a designation I could hold up for the world to see. I survived their teenage years, but more importantly—they survived me. Earning their college degrees my children stepped into the world of adulthood to pay off their college loans and find their purpose in life. That Saturday in May as I sat on my patio, I grieved over my job loss and wondered what I was supposed to be doing with my life now that my children were grown and on their own.

Kirsty, my eldest, was beautiful both inside and out. The soft, natural curl of her mahogany-colored hair framed her face and accentuated her warm, brown eyes…eyes that reminded me of my mother's. Petite in stature her five foot two inch frame could not compare with the size of her will. Her quiet demeanor and determination prevailed in a family of extraverts competing for attention. Completing her master's degree in occupational therapy, she had worked the entire time she was in college, went on to graduate school and had graduated with honors before marrying her college sweetheart. On the hottest day of the year, as the thermometer pushed 111 degrees in the shade, my daughter and her fiance were married at Fountain Park in Dallas beneath a canopy of cypress trees surrounded by cascading waters. Kirsty's husband Warren was a talented graphic artist and art director and had accepted a job in San Francisco. Newly married and eager to create a life of their own, they were packing their belongings for their move to California. The weekend of July 4th, barely five weeks away, they would be on their way.

Aubrey, my middle child and only son, had graduated with a degree in construction management and was an officer in the US Army. With an enormous heart, my handsome son, towered over all of us in height and learned early in life that he could use his size and facial expressions to keep others at any distance he desired. Engaging and funny his unmatched sense of loyalty was part and parcel of his personality. And his genuine love for those he cared about earned him life-long friends and respect from his troops. His honesty also earned him an approving smile from his dog's veterinarian and a glare from the minister doing their pre-marital counseling sessions when my son compared the depth of his love for his fiancée Angie to his love for Brandy—his dog.

That morning as I looked across my backyard, I thought about my son and what life must be like for him. He had been deployed during operation Iraqi Freedom in March and was in charge of a large contingent of soldiers. We had been told that his deployment would last another 10 to 12 months. When he would be home again, no one knew for sure.

Bridget, my youngest, was a runner. Athletic and bright, my exotic green-eyed daughter was a beauty as well and had been chosen homecoming queen at her brother's school. But it was not her beauty that earned her a scholarship to Stanford University; it was her intellect and talent. Graduating with a degree in civil and environmental engineering, Bridget made a courageous decision to follow her dreams and go to New York City. Rethinking her career path, she stepped into the world of finance merging her love for construction and math into a career in real estate investment. Watching her balance her budget those first two months in a city that along with the IRS demanded over half her earnings in taxes, I noted an ironic parallel in our lives and teased her that she had gone to New York City to experience poverty after graduating from university, while I had joined the Peace Corps to experience it. The teasing ended abruptly on September 11, 2001 after Bridget stood beside her coworkers looking out the window of their office building as smoke billowed from the twin towers of the World Trade Center and the attacks of 9/11 changed the city and our nation forever. Unflinching and courageous, my daughter became her own woman and made the decision to stay in New York City and make Manhattan her home.

With the children grown, life without the responsibility of raising them and attending to their needs was certainly easier and definitely quieter. Sometimes I longed for the excitement they brought into my life, but the truth was, I felt relieved. I was happy for them and experienced a sense of freedom that I had not experienced in over 20 years. I had been looking forward to this time in my life when they were on their own...when my youngest was out of college, and I could slow down and be a little selfish with my time and my resources. There was so much I wanted to do; there was so much I wanted to see.

Sunlight filtering through the leaves of the maple tree danced across the patio and distracted me from thoughts of my children. Memories of my manager's words that I tried to ignore slipped back into my consciousness, and I swallowed hard wishing the tea I drank could soothe the thickening knot in my stomach and somehow make it all go away.

Two weeks before, blinded by my own sense of self-importance, I had bounded up three flights of stairs to the executive suites fully confident that a promotion lay in wait. The time was 4:30 in the afternoon; the date was Friday, May 15, 2003. I wasn't entirely foolish. I knew that new business decisions and an upcoming corporate reorganization could very well put my position at risk. Catching the negative thought midstream, I eliminated it quickly and focused on my aspirations and dreams. Visualizing my career goals, I focused my energy on thinking positive thoughts and was confident that my achievements and the long hours I had put in at work spoke for themselves. If the reorganization did eliminate my job, I was confident that a transfer to one of our sister companies in Connecticut or New Jersey would be the next career step with the company.

I respected my manager and liked working for him. Beyond his creativity and boyish good looks, Larry's skill set included an ability to communicate strategy and build a great team. In addition, he was one of the few bosses I knew who genuinely cared about his employees and wanted them to grow both personally and professionally. Opening the door to his office that afternoon, he seemed a bit pensive as he stepped aside and invited me to sit down. Noticing the neat stack of papers on the table behind him, my heart felt a sudden sense of dread. Even before he spoke, I knew what he was going to say. Trying to be gentle, he prefaced his message, "This is the most difficult part of my job...." He didn't have to say another word. He was delivering a message I didn't want to hear. The papers on the table behind him were my release papers, and his job was to tell me that I was being laid off from my job...let go...separated from the company. It didn't matter what words he used, my livelihood...my income...the job I loved was going away.

I had known that this moment was a possibility, but in my optimism, bolstered by pride, I didn't believe that I would be one of the employees laid off. For that reason alone, feelings of embarrassment and foolishness interwoven with a compelling desire to run out of his office threatened my composure. Convinced that no man who faced what I was facing would be caught crying, I suppressed the tears that welled up inside me. Larry continued speaking, but I heard little more than muffled sounds and a smattering of words, like "severance" and something about making "doctor appointments" as soon as possible because I would soon be on "COBRA". Quite honestly, other than those words, I heard very little of what he said and understood less. Instead, I was thinking about what I would say to my children and what I would tell my coworkers.

Steeling my emotions, I forced my eyes to look at Larry as though I were listening, but I never really saw him. In the periphery of my vision, beyond the window in his office, I saw the blue Texas sky offering me an escape and my imagination took over. I couldn't remember the last time I had taken a casual walk beneath broad skies or listened to birds singing in the branches of trees. Then, in the midst of my thoughts, I noticed a faint tingling deep inside and the tingling grew to a quiver and the quiver to a rattle. Adrenalin sloshed through the deepest recesses of my being and took residence deep inside the marrow of my bones. I began to shiver involuntarily, and I clenched my teeth silently praying that I could stop them from chattering. I was cold...frigid cold...so cold that even a blanket could not warm me. My body was in shock!

In minutes, he was finished. Politely, Larry pushed back his chair and stood up. I still had two weeks to work. May 30 would be my last day with the company.

Escorting me out of his office and passed the familiar cubicles of the legal department, there was nothing more to say, yet Larry continued to talk. His heart seemed to be in his words as he repeated repeated himself. As his words registered for the second time, I suddenly questioned his sincerity and wondered how something that had the potential to destroy my life was somehow all about him. Suppressing a rising urge to lash out, I looked at him and wondered if he had the faintest understanding of the impact of his words on me. It was not his livelihood that was going away; it was mine.

Where the words came from, I really don't know, but intrinsically, I knew that losing my job was about something much more important than the work I had been performing the past three and a half years. It was about returning to a promise that I had made to God when I was still a teenager...a promise to serve Him. Suddenly calm and confident, the words slipped out, "Trust me, Larry. This is not about you; this is about God and me."

I could not explain it at the time, but somehow, I knew that what was happening was no accident. I had hit a wall. And deep within me, I knew that God was redirecting my path and was holding me accountable for an unfulfilled promise that I had made as a teenager...a commitment to serve him. I had not always been the most compliant sheep in the flock and had had my fair share of back-sliding, but this much I knew, God had my attention. I was not about to go wandering off to spend another 40 years wandering in a desert wilderness of my own creation. without taking time to consider God's part in my life and His plans for my future. I had done that before, and I had no intention of doing it again.

I walked down the stairs, stepped into my cubicle and checked my messages. I had much to do over the course of the next two weeks. May 30, my last day, would be here soon enough. When I left my cubicle for the last time, I was determined there would be no surprises for anyone. My files would be in perfect order; my vendors would know whom to contact when I was gone; and everyone would have access to everything they needed to continue without me.

For the first time that I could remember in three and a half years, I put away everything on my desk. And despite the initial shock that my job was going away, I went home unencumbered with worry...confident that another job, a better job than the one I had known and loved the last three and a half years was waiting for me out there. My job was to find it.

The old adage, God helps those who help themselves had been drilled into me as a child and young adult. I believed in the American dream of hard work and determination, of goal setting and self help. Growing up, I practiced it with zeal and conscientiously worked hard to earn my just rewards.

I bought into the idea that being good, knowledgeable and talented earned me the right to a good job, a nicer house and a new car. In my short-sighted efforts to be self-sufficient, I was busy all the time. The truth was, I had been crazy busy. My meeting with Larry changed all that in a heartbeat. Like hitting a wall going ninety to nothing, Larry's announcement stopped me in my tracks. And, in a split second, my dreams and everything I had worked so hard to achieve so that I could be self-sufficient and take care of care of myself and family were stripped away. My job...my income...my livelihood was gone.

Believing in the American way was not the only thing I believed in. Believing I knew what it meant to be a Christian, I had come to the conclusion long ago that being in church each Sunday, volunteering with the youth group and helping those less fortunate was a measure of my goodness and faithfulness. I had developed the naïve belief that because I believed in God and was a good person who taught Sunday School and did good things for others, God would look kindly on my efforts and protect my family and me from difficulties that others faced. In those days, I had no understanding that there was little correlation between believing in God, doing good things for others and having an easier life.

Over the course of the next three months, despite telling Larry that the lay-off was "between God and me," I was about to come face-to-face with the unabridged version of the truth—I believed in God, but I had no idea who this God I professed to believe in really was. Most of my life, I had been able to rely on my ingenuity and self-will to get through the difficult times and achieve the goals I set out to achieve. The fine line between God's will and free will was blurred, and I was about to learn more about God than my pride-filled heart could ever imagine.

... there lived a man whose name was Job. This man was blameless and upright; he feared God and shunned evil. He had seven sons and three daughters, and he owned seven thousand sheep, three thousand camels, five hundred yoke of oxen and five hundred donkeys, and had a large number of servants. He was the greatest man above all the people of the East.

Job 1: 1-3

3

The First Messenger

The First Messenger

Whatever the reason, I never seemed to identify with the beautiful stories in the Bible about women like Esther and Ruth. Perhaps it was because they were rarely talked about in church when I grew up. I did, however, love the stories about men like Joseph and David...Samson and Moses. I admired their strength and character, their determination and perseverance. There was much for me to learn about Esther and Ruth, their strength and character, their femininity and beauty that the Davids and Samsons, the men of the Bible could not teach me.

There were, however, other men in the Bible whose stories and character seemed somehow uninviting and less heroic to me. One such man was a man named Job. Job was a wealthy man who loved God. Proving to Satan that Job was a righteous man, God allowed Satan to take away Job's flocks, his possessions, his children, and his health. In the midst of his trials, Job never turned his back on God even as one messenger after another delivered not just bad news, but devastating news that culminated in Job losing everything of worldly value in his life: his wealth, his children and his health. In sorrow over his losses, Job mourned by tearing his clothing and covering himself in ashes, a common practice among the people in those days.

The very idea of a grown man sitting in ashes praising God was foreign to me and not just counter intuitive, but counterproductive to all that I understood from my culture as a little girl growing up among Midwest pragmatists. Over the years, I had been taught by well-meaning people to hide my pain and grief. I was neither able nor willing to understand a man like Job, a grief stricken man who praised God in the midst of tragedy and loss.

As I grew into adulthood, I discovered that some losses were easier to get over than others. The unexpected death of my father crushed me. And the loss of not one, but two failed marriages had all but destroyed my confidence as a woman and my ability to build a committed relationship—even with girl friends.

The lay-off was a bit different than other losses in my life. This loss threatened my basic needs for food, shelter and clothing—my very survival.

I imagine Job was stunned by the news the first messenger delivered that his oxen and donkeys had been stolen. Like Job, I was stunned when my first messenger, my manager, delivered the news that I was being laid off.

I do not envy a messenger's responsibility; it is not easy to deliver bad news. Little did I know that not unlike the messengers in the story of Job, other messengers were on their way; I had only met my first.

While he was still speaking, another [messenger] came and said, "The fire of God fell from heaven and burned up the sheep and the servants, and consumed them; I alone have escaped to tell you.

Job 1:16

The Second Messenger

The Second Messenger

Plano, Texas
June 2003

Unencumbered with working late, I woke early and walked to the park as the sun rose and birds built their nests. I watched as mallards with iridescent green feathers directed their mates to nest under the shade of the crepe myrtles near the pond where their newly-hatched ducklings would soon float across its shallow waters.

The first two weeks following the lay-off, I focused my days around honing my resume and applying for jobs. My desire to get back into the full-swing of working as soon as possible motivated me to arrange delayed doctor appointments. My long overdue mammogram and doctor's appointment to examine an annoying little cyst on my breast was scheduled for that afternoon.

The Texas heat was just gearing up when I turned my car into the parking lot of the diagnostic center. Pink begonias blossomed along the walkway that led to the entrance of the breast surgeon's office conveniently located in the same building as the mammography center.

I had known about the hard, pea-sized cyst on my left breast for almost two years. The cyst, located just under the skin of the areola about a half inch from the tip of the nipple, caused no pain, but displayed the disconcerting signs of an unwanted discharge from time to time. Several doctors had examined it, and all had reassured me that it was a papilloma, a noncancerous cyst consisting of fibrous tissue and blood vessels. Lodged in the milk duct of my left breast, the medical professionals had concluded that the papilloma was the culprit...the source of the inflammation and discharge.

Over the course of a couple years, after being reassured following each visit that the papilloma was benign and showed no signs of any change, the doctors at the diagnostic center continued to recommend that I have the cyst checked by a medical professional every three to six months. After the first couple of exams confirmed that the cyst had not changed, I took it upon myself to stretch my check ups from every six months to every nine months. As the months past, I convinced myself that the cyst, as small and innocuous as it was, was really a not threat at all. Dismissing the professionals recommendations as over-cautious, I used my busyness at work and commitments to my family as an excuse to avoid my checkups for over a year.

When the technician completed the mammogram and sonogram, I dressed, crossed the foyer and entered my breast surgeon's waiting room confident that the results would once again show no significant changes. However, Dr. Hampe, my breast surgeon, gave me news quite different from what I expected. The cyst had changed in size, and he recommended it be removed and biopsied as soon as possible.

The following week, I went to the hospital for outpatient surgery. The procedure was over quickly, and before noon, my friend Becky drove me home to rest.

The next morning as I stood in front the mirror and gently lifted the gauze, I was amazed by what I saw and pleased to discover just how skilled my surgeon was; the incision was barely noticeable. Dr. Hampe had removed the cyst and glued the two-inch incision back in place with such precision that even I could see that there would be no tell-tale scar.

Three days after the surgery, I received a letter in the mail, opened it and read the results of the sonogram and mammogram. The results showed no evidence of any abnormality or cancer. Relieved, I focused all my energy on my job search. Consumed with writing the final draft of my resume and connecting with headhunters and recruiters, I ignored any interruptions that might distract me from my goals.

Over the next couple of days, my breast surgeon's nurse followed-up with telephone calls and left several messages in an effort to set up an appointment for a post-surgery examination. Between the letter I received in the mail that there was "no evidence of cancer" and the rapid healing of the incision, I assumed her calls were routine. Engrossed in applying for jobs and getting caught up on chores, I dismissed her calls as unimportant and gave her neither the time nor the courtesy of a returned call. On the seventh day, as my answering machine picked up the call, I heard the nurse's voice on the machine. Polite, but clearly concerned that I had not yet returned her calls to set up my post surgical appointment, I listened as she began to leave yet another message.

Embarrassed by my lack of courtesy, I picked up the phone mid-message with a lame apology about being exceptionally busy. The nurse explained that protocol required a post-op visit. Still trying to avoid the appointment, I insisted that I was fine and the incision had healed nicely. With inexplicable patience, she became politely more resolute until I agreed to come into the office at the end of the week.

I arrived at Dr. Hampe's office promptly at 4:30 in the afternoon; the date was Friday, June 13, 2003 - exactly two weeks to the day following my last day of work. The nurse welcomed me and walked me back to the examination room. Moments later, the surgeon entered the room and asked how I was feeling. He examined the incision and assured me that it was healing nicely. Pausing momentarily, he took a slight step backward. Soft spoken and kind, Dr. Hampe chose his words carefully as he shared the results of the pathology report in the gentlest possible manner that he could. The cyst was a small tumor, an estrogen positive, inductile carcinoma. Stunned by his words, I looked in his eyes with disbelief. I had breast cancer!

For the second time in two weeks, I was shaken to the core. Unstoppable waves of adrenaline, cold like the icy waters of the North Atlantic, washed through my body and deep into the marrow of my bones. I searched for words, but the pounding of my heart drowned out all effort to speak.

Making every effort to remain calm and composed in front of my doctor and his nurse, I did my best not to panic as a tidal wave of fear flooded my senses. Like a drowning man... unable to breath...unable to call for help, I could neither speak nor dismiss the fear. In the recesses of my being, I struggled to contain the fear that rushed through me. Once again, I screamed silently holding back my emotions long enough for my brain to come to my rescue as if logic and reason could reverse the diagnosis, "I don't have a job! I can't afford to have cancer!" In shock and denial, I searched for a lifeline of hope and struggled to speak, "...but the letter..."

"What letter?" he inquired with a puzzled expression. We looked at one another, both of us unsure about what the other was referencing.

I reached in my purse and pulled out the letter that had come in the mail. The radiologists report concluded there was "no evidence of any abnormality" and came with a recommendation that I schedule a follow-up mammogram and sonogram in six months. In my eagerness to believe that all was well, I overlooked the signature on the letter. The letter had not come from my breast surgeon; it had been signed by the radiologist who worked for the diagnostic center located next door to my surgeon's office.

My breast surgeon and I had been referring to the results of two entirely different reports. I had been talking about the results of the mammogram and sonogram performed several days before I had gone to the hospital for the biopsy; my surgeon had been relaying the results of the biopsy, a pathology report that examined the breast tissue specimens and provided a more accurate analysis than either the mammogram or sonogram.

Despite the initial shock that the tumor was cancerous, there was some good news. The doctors assured me that the odds were in my favor. With early detection, the size of the tumor and type of breast cancer that I was diagnosed with meant that the chance of a metastasis, the spread of the cancer to another place in my body, was less than three percent. With those odds, I had the advantage. Early detection meant treatment would be less invasive and less taxing on my body. My chances for a full recovery appeared to be extremely high.

Although the tissue around the tumor had appeared free of cancer, the pathology report stated otherwise. Before I could meet with the oncologist to explore treatment options, I needed to have a second biopsy, this time in pursuit of clear, cancer-free margins at the tumor site. The nurse scheduled a second outpatient surgery for me at a nearby hospital.

My concerns began to grow. I sensed that I was not going to be able to pretend that the breast cancer was less serious than it was. Brewing in my intuition was a growing awareness that a battle was about to take place. Already, my suspicions were coming to fruition.

I had watched my friends Barb, Sandy and Carmen triumph through their surgeries and cancer treatments. I had known that my sister Lynne had gone through not one, but two bouts of breast cancer. All had been stoic. All had been examples of courage, and all had survived. Their lives were living proof that women can and do survive breast cancer. I knew little about breast cancer, but I did know that there are many kinds and stages of breast cancer and that many women do not survive the disease. My mother's friend, Evy, was the first woman I knew who died from the disease. My Aunt Myrtle and Aunt Winnie were next in line. I tried to lessen my fears by convincing myself that they had not had the advantage of current research, new medicines and new treatment protocols.

I focused on the positive, the fact that early detection and treatment options gave me hope for a cure. I was convinced that like my friends and my sister before me, I would survive. I wasn't going to wait for my doctors to tell me what to do. I decided that I would research and read every reliable resource I could find that might be useful in helping me beat the cancer. Unlike some of my friends, I wanted to know everything. I wanted to know about the disease, the treatment and the possible contraindications. I knew my diet had been lousy and was determined to change it – eat healthy, purchase organic foods and avoid sugar. I committed then and there to give up processed foods and start juicing with fresh vegetables.

I knew that getting well required both personal discipline and an investment of both time and money. Now, more than ever, I needed health insurance and steady income. My COBRA coverage was available, but paying my share of the costs for health insurance required taking money out of my meager retirement account – something I wanted to avoid. I decided I needed to continue to apply for jobs and that if I ever expected to get hired, I would have to hide the fact that I had cancer from potential employers. Unemployed and diagnosed with cancer, I left the doctor's office in shock...sure that things couldn't get much worse.

Looking back at the story of Job, I am sure that when the second messenger told Job his sheep and servants had been consumed by a great fire from the sky, he didn't think things could get much worse. Like Job, my second messenger had arrived. My kind and caring breast surgeon had been my second messenger, delivering news that I had breast cancer. Like Job, I didn't think things could get much worse.

Two are better than one ...
if one falls down
his friends can help him up.

Ecclesiastes 4:9-10

5

Friends

Friends

Plano, Texas
July 2003

Before making any more decisions about treatment, I was determined to get a second opinion, and if necessary, I would get a third. Judy, a close friend who was a nurse, recommended Dr. Blumenschein. My daughter Kirsty and my friend Nance drove me to the doctor's office and waited with me to hear the second doctor's conclusions. Dr. Blumenschein agreed with Dr. Hampe's recommendations, And even more important to me was the specialist's assurance that Dr. Hampe was one of the best and had an excellent reputation among his colleagues. The trip had been worth it, the second doctor's assurance was exactly what I needed to hear.

I returned to Dr. Hampe's office ready to move forward with confidence that I was in good hands. I had several treatment options: a lumpectomy followed by radiation and possibly chemotherapy, a mastectomy of my left breast followed by radiation, or a bi-lateral mastectomy followed by chemotherapy. With input from the medical professionals and my sister Lynne, I decided to have both breasts removed and scheduled surgery for a bi-lateral mastectomy on July 22, 2003.

Two reasons led to my decision. First, I wanted to reduce the risk of the cancer returning. I had a family history of breast cancer. My sister, during her first bout with breast cancer, had opted to have a single, diseased breast removed. Five years later, Lynne was diagnosed with cancer in the breast that she did not have removed. I reasoned that removing both breasts was preventative and would reduce the chance of a recurrence.

Second, I wanted as few surgeries as possible. I disliked anesthesia, being out of control and the sluggish feeling that always followed me around for weeks after surgery. But the real reason I disliked anesthesia was that I was afraid. I was terrified that I would go to sleep and not wake up. My father had died during open heart surgery, not from the effects of anesthesia, but from other complications. Still, he never woke up, and we never got to say goodbye.

My sister had chosen not to do reconstructive surgery. She was not comfortable with the idea of putting man-made plastic or silicone in her body. Her husband of 35 years supported her decision fully, and I did too. However, I wasn't so certain I would follow in her footsteps. With a penchant for losing things, I imagined the worst case scenario, and the last thing I wanted to be concerned about was a prosthesis slipping out by some embarrassing turn of events and ending up at my dance partner's feet in the middle of the dance floor.

I had no problem having my breasts removed to prevent the spread of cancer, but I had other reservations. Still insecure from my failed marriages and still wanting so much to meet that one special someone, I wanted to feel as much like a woman as I could, and I wanted my breasts to look as much like a normal woman's breasts as they could. For me, that meant reconstructive surgery.

At the time, I didn't fully understand that underlying my motives to have reconstructive surgery was the stirring of my feminine heart. I still dreamed of wearing that one special dress, my preference, a beautiful strapless dress that made me feel like the captivating woman I wanted to be. I had no clue that deep inside my soul was the wounded heart of a woman waiting to be restored. Never for a moment did I consider that my journey with cancer would lead me to her or the reasons that I had banned her from my consciousness.

I found myself in a new place physically and emotionally. I might have been able to manage the job loss on my own, but the upcoming surgery and chemotherapy was something I was determined not do alone.

I had no immediate or extended family in the Dallas area to turn to. I had never considered the possibility, that I might one day need my children more than they needed me. Each had grown up and had responsibilities of their own. And each lived further away from Dallas than the other. My siblings, Lynne and Fred, and my nieces and nephews all lived over 1,200 miles away.

Without my immediate family's physical presence, I had to turn to others for support. Laying aside my pride and illusion of self-sufficiency, I reached out to the women in my Sunday School class at church—The Welcome Class. These women and their husbands were friends I trusted. They were friends who had been there for me in the past—

in good times and bad. And now, I needed them more than ever as my advocates; I needed them to listen to the doctors' recommendations and help me sort through the unfolding chaos and many decisions that had to be made. These women were my girl friends, the women upon whom I could depend to pray for me...women who would eagerly reach out to pick up a piece of the burden that was too big for me to carry alone.

We know that all things work together for good for those who love God, who are called according to his purpose.

Romans 8:28

The Mastectomy

The Mastectomy

Dallas, Texas
July 22, 2003

The searing Texas heat camped outside my hospital window. The date was Tuesday, July 22, 2003, the day of my mastectomy.

Inside the hospital room, bags of saline solution, antibiotics and morphine hung from tall, steel-gray stands at the head of my bed. Their contents dripped slowly through a maze of tubes into the needle embedded in my arm as I drifted in and out of consciousness to the distant murmuring of hushed voices.

The gentle touch and kind voice of a nurse nudged me to wake. "Susan, can you hear me? Susan, open your eyes."

I struggled to lift my eyelids against the lingering effects of the anesthesia. As the blur of faces slowly came into focus, a second voice whispered, "She's waking. Mom, you're doing fine." I searched the room to put my daughter's face with her voice. There at the end of my bed sat both my daughters, Kirsty and Bridget, the younger sister, the taller of the two, cradled in her older sister's lap

Making an effort to move my arm, I felt a sudden, painful pull from stitches that held multiple tubes securely between my ribs to drain the fluids from the surgical wounds. I sensed an unusual heaviness, like a weight pressing down on both sides of my chest just below my collar bone, a reminder that the plastic surgeon had inserted expanders that would be filled with saline solution to stretch the muscle for future breast reconstruction.

Responding to the nurse's commands, I felt her hand as she placed the morphine pump firmly into the palm of my own hand. Placing my thumb on a button, she spoke softly and clearly, "Susan, if you feel pain – just squeeze the button." As if on cue to the word pain, an intense ache seemed to rise from out of my chest. I pressed the button and drifted off to sleep, surrounded by my daughters and girl friends, comforted by their presence and soothing voices. The only one missing was my son Aubrey.

By afternoon, I was lucid enough to request my cell phone. I ask that it to be placed at my bedside so that I could answer quickly if my son called from overseas.

True to my expectation, the cell phone rang. I inhaled deeply and gathered all the strength I could muster to answer with a reassuring, upbeat voice. Because he was in a war zone, I feared for his safety and knew my son needed to be attentive to doing his job, not worrying about his mother. I pressed the talk button with confidence that the voice behind the unidentified number would be my son's. As the room quieted in anticipation of his call from half way around the world, I did my best to sound as normal as I could.

"Hello! This is Susan Abar," I said eagerly.

"Hello," responded the man at the other end. "This is Maverick's mother." Puzzled by the manly voice on the other end of the phone proclaiming to be someone's mother, I pulled the phone away from my ear and looked at the receiver wondering how someone who sounded so much like a man could be claiming to be someone's mother. The anesthetic had worn off enough for me to question whether it was my hearing or the lingering effects of anesthetic in my system.

I hesitated, "Excuse me? Would you repeat your name again?"

The voice on the other end of the phone responded, "This is Maverick Smothers. I'm calling you to see if you might be interested in talking to me about a position with our company in Redmond, Washington."

Not about to let an opportunity to get my foot in the door slip away, I took my hand off the button to the morphine pump and motioned for my friends to leave the room. One-by-one they filed into the hallway, allowing me to concentrate and answer each question as if I'd been sitting at home all morning prepping for the phone interview.

As the conversation ended, my friend, Tina, cracked the door open and inquired on behalf of the others, "Was that an interview?" I nodded my head to the affirmative. With little energy left and the pain escalating, I pressed the button to the morphine pump, "I have an interview with the hiring manager in two weeks."

My friends and family look at me incredulously with raised eyebrows. Someone in the room began to snicker, and then another, and another... each trying to hide their amusement... each convinced that the morphine was in high gear. Moments later the morphine did kick in, and I drifted off to sleep with the knowledge of their presence calming my fears and the melodic sweetness of their laughter lifting my spirits.

Our life as mortals is but a breath in length. We are no different than the flowers – beautiful and delicate, sturdy and hearty – dropping petals one by one, until the last breeze, the last breath, takes away the last petal, and we return to dust.

Susan Abar
April 23, 2007

The Third Messenger

7

The Third Messenger

Plano, Texas
August 2003

Two weeks after the mastectomy, I was scheduled to meet with the hiring manager from Redmond while he was in Plano on business. Getting dressed for the interview, I ran into a slight problem related to the surgery. To allow fluids to drain from the surgical wounds created by the mastectomy and reduce swelling, the surgeon had inserted three tubes, each about three feet in length. Stitched securely in place between two ribs, all three tubes protruded out of the sides of my rib cage: two on my left side and one on my right. Attached to the end of each tube was a tear-drop shaped bulb that collected the fluids that drained from the wounds. The surgeon had assured me that when the wounds began to heal and stopped draining the tubes and cue-ball size bulbs would be removed, but the wounds had not yet healed.

Showing up for the interview was easy; hiding the tubes and the bulbs under my clothing was not. Unable to lift my arms above my head, Tina came over to my house mid morning to help me dress. We used surgical tape to secure the tubes to my sides and abdomen. Then, I came up with what I thought was a rather cute, if not ingenious idea. Rather than let the bulbs dangle at my sides, I decided to hide the bulbs inside the cups of my bra! When Tina wasn't looking, I did just that. What I thought was an ingenious idea was actually not a wise one. What I had not considered was the effect of gravity. Placing the bulbs higher than the wound site prevented gravity from doing its job which was to allow fluids from the surgical wounds to drain out of the tubes and down into the bulbs. At the time, I had no idea that my ingenious idea could have had disastrous short-term and long-term side effects.

The interview with the hiring manager went well. As a result, I received still another invitation to interview with senior leaders at the corporate headquarters located in Redmond, Washington. The recruiter and her assistant scheduled my interview for Friday, August 29 and made travel arrangements for me to fly to Washington and rent a car on the day before the interview.

I returned home from the interview in Plano exhausted, but excited and pleased… excited by the prospect that I might have a job soon and pleased by my ability to execute my plans. For two hours over lunch, I answered every question. I knew my stuff, and I knew it well. Feeling quite smug and more than a little full of myself, I left the interviewing certain that the manager had no idea that I was not in perfect health. Removing the tape from the tubes and taking the bulbs out of my bra, I let them hang where they were supposed to hang – below my waist. I put on my pajamas and crawled into bed too exhausted to move.

I considered getting through the mastectomy to be one milestone on my journey with breast cancer. I viewed chemotherapy, reconstructive surgery and follow-up treatment as other milestones. In my mind's eye, I had carefully placed those milestones as markers so that I could track my progress in achieving my goal: to be five years out of treatment and cancer-free.

Taking my first step to check off the chemotherapy milestone, I walked into North Texas Oncology as the sliding glass doors opened with a full head of hair and my girlfriend Nance at my side. The previous two and a half months had been a challenge, but with the surgery behind me, I was mentally prepared to do what needed to be done to be free of cancer. I wanted to live and if living meant having my breasts surgically removed, losing my hair and being bald, that was okay by me.

Waiting in the small examination room for my oncologist, Dr. Christopher Stokoe, Nance and I busied ourselves with small talk about my upcoming interview in Redmond. I was excited about the prospect, not only because I knew that I could do the job and do it well, but because the doctors had assured me that excellent cancer treatment centers in the Seattle/Redmond area could provide me with chemotherapy and any treatment I might need. At this point, everything seemed to be falling in place.

Despite my determined optimism, my doctors were very cautious. Following my mastectomy and the routine dissection of the sentinel node, another pathology report had revealed that cancer the size of a pinhead had rooted itself into one of my lymph nodes, hence additional lymph nodes and tissue needed to be reevaluated. The oncologist explained that the metastasis meant that the doctors needed to run additional tests and that the original protocol for treatment that we had discussed earlier would, in all likelihood, change.

It seemed that every which way I turned my bout with breast cancer seemed to be defying the odds. Despite a three per cent chance of a lymph node testing positive for the type of slow-growing breast cancer I had, the pathology report on the lymph node confirmed I had not escaped cancer's tentacles. The cancer had metastasized! To rule out any suspicion that cancer existed elsewhere in my body, my oncologist ordered not one but two sets of bone and soft tissue scans on two different days.

Nance drove me to my appointment with the oncologist to get the results and make certain that I thoroughly understood the protocol for chemotherapy. Dr. Stokoe walked into the examination room and acknowledged both of us. Sitting down he placed my ever-thickening file on the laminated counter top and asked, "How are you feeling?"

Trying to remain positive, I made a light-hearted joke about the surgery and possible future uses for the three plastic bulbs and the tubes still wired to my rib cage. Noticing his unusually somber demeanor, I finished what I was saying and waited quietly as he cleared his throat. He seemed to pause as if searching for just the right words – but there were no right words for what was coming. As he spoke, he used two words, pancreas and mass, in the same sentence, and as he did shock waves rolled through my body like a tsunami. I looked at him in utter disbelief as his words dissipated into unintelligible white noise and my senses numbed once again.

My vision tunneled, turning colorful wall prints into monochromatic shades of gray—gray like a Michigan winter's day gripped in bone-chilling cold. But I wasn't in Michigan; I was in Texas where the sun shines brightly, and the August heat forces people to seek refuge behind closed doors in air conditioned rooms. The windowless walls seemed to close in around me, and I gasped in an effort to breathe. Memories of my mother raced through my mind, and I remembered the look on her face as hope turned into hopelessness, and her beautiful brown eyes grew strange and distant when her doctor said there was nothing more they could do. Feeling trapped, as if the room was closing in upon me, I excused myself to go to the rest room.

Nance told me later that when I left the room, Dr. Stokoe turned to her, slowly shook his head from side-to-side before speaking in a tone that reflected sorrow, "Your friend is going to need you now, more than ever. This really isn't good."

It was not the restroom I needed, but a safe haven—a place to escape and be alone with my thoughts. My stomach recoiled as I stood in front of the basin and turned on the faucets. I looked in the mirror at my own reflection and remembered my mother's eyes, distant and dark with fear. Peering at my own eyes in the reflection before me, I noticed a startling similarity between my mother's eyes and my own. My eyes, normally light in color were suddenly haunting and dark like my mother's. I knew what she felt that day when she learned the news that she had a mass on her pancreas and there was nothing more the doctor's could do. Tearlessly, I wondered, "How much time did I have left? Would it be seven weeks like my mother? And her father before her?"

Mother's father had time to travel on the train with my grandmother from Michigan to Missouri to say good-by to his brother and his extended family in the state in which he had grown up. He returned to his home in Michigan, jaundiced and unable to eat. Within weeks my grandmother rode the train south again, this time to bury her dead husband in the family plot as was his wish.

In the beginning, Mother had hope. It had been over thirty years since her father had passed away, and she felt certain that with over thirty years of advances in cancer research the medical community must have made progress in treating and curing pancreatic cancer. Entering the hospital at the University of Michigan, she was prepared to do whatever it took, but there was nothing doctors could do – no tests, no experimental drugs, no surgery – nothing. The mass had progressed too far; it had invaded her liver and was already blocking the bile duct. Early in the morning on the last day of May, my mother passed away in her own bed, in her own home, as was her desire.

I washed my hands and returned to the examination room to face my third messenger. Nance and Dr. Stokoe looked up as I walked in the door. Nance's face was pale, and it was clear that Dr. Stokoe was deeply bothered by the message he had just delivered. With a heavy heart, he offered me a thread of hope and referred me to a surgeon who specialized in a surgical procedure called a Whipple. The surgeon who specialized in the Whipple would be able to tell me whether or not removing my pancreas would be a viable option for me.

I remembered my plans to travel to Redmond for the upcoming interview scheduled for the last weekend in August. My best laid plans were falling apart.

Subsequent visits with the surgeon who was scheduled to remove my pancreas were disconcerting and left me questioning whether or not I wanted surgery at all. With each question that I asked about the Whipple procedure and its outcome, the surgeon appeared more and more annoyed. In his haste to dismiss my questions, I felt his growing disdain and perceived him as prideful and arrogant—lacking not in beside manner, but in compassion and maturity. During my fourth visit, I realized that I had given the surgeon every opportunity to prove to me that he valued me and cared about me as a person. Sitting in his office, I felt more like an object that would be used to demonstrate his surgical prowess and less like a patient of dignity and worth who sought his surgical expertise so that I might have a few more months of life to love my children and say good-by to my family and friends.

Tina and Nance alternated taking me to the surgeon. During my fourth visit, Nance accompanied me. As we left my appointment, I turned to her and asked her if she thought I should proceed with surgery. She responded that the only opinion that mattered was my own.

Discernment, that deep sense of knowing that comes only from God, set in. I glanced down at the floor and back up at Nance. Bowing my head and shaking it side-to-side, I responded, "I can't do it." She nodded in silent agreement.

Waiting for the elevator, Nance's cell phone interrupted the silence. One of the ministers from our church had been visiting patients in the hospital adjoining the doctor's office and was calling to see if I was available and would like to talk. I responded with a nod and barely intelligible whisper, "Yes."

The elevator bounced ever-so-slightly, and the steel doors opened. Stepping off the elevator and into a hallway, Nance led the way. Lush, green tropical plants populated the atrium in the hospital's foyer where we stood and watched the familiar face of our minister as he approached. Greeting us warmly, Nance stepped aside as he invited me to sit on the wooden bench to talk.

Experienced dealing with sickness and death, his spiritual guidance was welcome and his presence was comforting. We sat on the bench talking about my illness and my circumstance. Following a moment of silence he asked me, "What are you praying for?"

I knew exactly what I was praying for, but was afraid to tell him out of fear that this learned pastor would judge my prayer as self-serving and frivolous. I was praying that God would grant me one special moment—the opportunity to see my son and his fiancée married and dance at their wedding still nine months away. Already mourning the thought of weddings I would never see and grandchildren I would never hold, I prayed that the doctors had found the disease early enough that I might live until May.

Embarrassed by what I considered to be a selfish prayer, I lowered my voice to a whisper, "I'm praying to live long enough to dance at my son's wedding." Without ever saying the word death, my prayer was an acknowledgement that the end of my life as I knew it was eminent. Neither of us spoke for what seemed like a very long time. He pulled in a long slow breath and I prepared to listen. He spoke with the assurance of a man who knew a God that I did not know, "I'm praying for a miracle."

Taken aback, I looked at him with a puzzled expression. The thought of praying for a miracle had never crossed my mind, and I questioned if I had actually heard the word "miracle" come from his mouth. The words kept rolling over and over in my head as if I had never heard the word miracle before in my life. The idea of praying for a miracle seemed selfish to me and in my mind's eye, miracles were for the leper and the blind man, for Moses and for Lazareth. I thought miracles were stories about supernatural healing that took place only in the Bible. I could not fathom that miracles existed in today's world. But if they did, it was hard for me to imagine that God would spend a miracle on a woman like me. Still, deep inside, thoughts of a miracle began to germinate in my mind, and I began to pray. Little did I know that others who knew me were already praying, interceding on my behalf with prayers for a miracle.

Before we left, our minister taught me about breath prayers...little prayers...short enough to be completed in single breath. As the months and weeks progressed, those breath prayers would bring me peace in the face of many challenges.

Still in denial and unready to believe that there was no hope for a cure, I left the hospital in Dallas and made several important commitments to myself. First, I would identify every medical community that was a frontrunner in the latest research and treatment of pancreatic cancer and travel anywhere in the country to get their expert opinion. And second, I would not reveal to anyone other than my doctors, my closest friends and my immediate family, any more information until I had exhausted every avenue in front of me and knew the facts about my condition and the disease. And third, I would continue with my plans to travel to Redmond, Washington as if I was perfectly healthy. The interview with the hiring manager's team was scheduled for Friday, August 29, 2003 at the company's corporate offices only days away. The interview gave me something positive upon which to focus my energy; it gave me hope that I still had a future.

⸙

   Job's third messenger arrived on the heels of the second messenger, terrified by what he had seen and the slaughter he had escaped, burdened by the message he was charged to carry to Job—a message that a tribe from the north had come into Job's camp and killed all of his servants and stolen all 3,000 of his camels.

   I was beginning to see the story of Job and his messengers in a whole new light. I knew of the story of Job, a man who praised the Lord in the midst of enormous adversity; however, I had never considered the strength and courage that was required of his messengers who brought the devastating news they were charged to deliver.

   Like Job's third messenger, Dr. Stokoe was my third messenger. My job was gone. I had breast cancer and now a mass on my pancreas. Like Job, I had seen the pain in the eyes of my messenger as he searched my own. And I felt the ached in his heart and heard the strain in his voice as he imparted the devastating news he did not want to deliver.

We turn to God for help when our foundations are shaking, only to learn that it is God who is shaking them.

Charles C. West

The Interview

8

The Interview

Redmond, Washington
Friday, August 29, 2003

I have never understood why one person dies and another lives; why one person suffers tragedy and the other little or none at all. I have wondered why the greedy and the dishonest gather wealth at the expense of the powerless, knowing others sit hungry and homeless. In my questioning, I have learned that there are times when life is more challenging and difficult than we could imagine. The fact remains...life is unfair, and we don't always get what we plan for or work for.

Being laid off from work, diagnosed with breast cancer and a fast growing mass on my pancreas was mind boggling. I struggled to understand how the doctors could tell me I had a rapidly growing tumor growing inside me when I felt fine. Desperately trying to dismiss the idea of Stage IV cancer from my mind, my thoughts ranged from thinking I was much too young to die to rationalizing that I had much too much to live for to have terminal cancer. The rationalizations continued and my emotions raged, but in the end there was nothing I could do to change what was happening to me. Coming face to face with the fact that there was nothing I could do to change my circumstances, I began to realize that within my circumstances I could change.

Owning up to the fact that I would never be able to change the doctor's diagnosis or my circumstances, I made a conscious decision to change my mind-set. I realized I could live my life focused on what I thought I should do or I could believe that God was doing something far greater that I could not comprehend. As each challenge I faced magnified itself beyond my ability to cope, it became easier to seek God for what I needed and put my self-determination and ego on the shelf. Knowing that God gave order to the universe in the midst of chaos meant He was the same God in whom I could trust regardless of my circumstance. Conceiving of a God who brought order in the midst of chaos had once seemed much too deep and complex for me to consider. Now facing my own death, the scriptures that told me about this God of mine brought me enormous peace. And there was more that I wanted to know about Him...more that I needed to know about this God who was in control of everything including the day of my birth and the day of my death. Proverbs 3:5-6, "Trust in the Lord with all your heart and lean not upon your own understanding. In all ways acknowledge Him and He will direct your path..." was the answer to my question, and I no longer needed to ask, "Why me?"

So why had I been compelled to travel 1,800 miles from my home in Texas to interview for a job in the Pacific Northwest? I had no answer at the time, only the compelling need to go. Eventually, I would understand that traveling to Redmond was the only thing in my life over which I thought I had any shred of control.

The weather in Redmond was beautiful when I arrived, an anomaly, pure sunshine in a city known for dreary gray skies and rain. The day after the interview, in the tranquility of the morning with no need to get up and no responsibility to own, I lay on the bed in my hotel room and drifted in and out of sleep. Waking slowly, the memory of that day in Dr. Stokoe's office never quite left me, and I wondered out of curiosity and fear, "How many days did I have left?" I considered a multitude of questions that had no answers. "How would I spend those days? Would I spend my days searching for a cure – taking drugs and chemotherapy? Or would I spend my days healing wounds?" Intrinsically, I knew time was the most significant thing I had left. And that time would provide me the opportunity to deal with wounds from my past. I still had time to ask for forgiveness from those whom I had wronged and to forgive those who had wronged me. As the morning light seeped into the hotel room, the words of Robert Frost slipped into my consciousness.

> *Two paths diverged in a yellow wood…*
> *And both that morning equally lay*
> *In leaves no step had trodden black.*
> *Yet knowing how way leads on to way,*
> *I doubted if I should ever come back…*

The shuffling of feet and the quiet closure of a door outside my hotel room signaled another guest's departure, providing the distraction I needed from my thoughts.

Up until now, neither the lay-off nor the mastectomy had crushed my spirit; I had been able to rebound. But everything changed that afternoon when Dr. Stokoe told me about the mass on my pancreas.

Before learning of the diagnosis of the mass on my pancreas, I was convinced that I could balance chemotherapy for breast cancer and a new job in a state far away from friends and family. Courageous, well-meaning women before me had set the standard, and I had thought I could follow in their footsteps. The women I had known who had walked this path before me had hidden their bald heads under beautiful wigs and brightly colored scarves. And they had hidden their fears behind smiling masks of determination, hope and faith. I had wrongly concluded their attempts to normalize their lives through regular work schedules, surgeries, radiation, and chemotherapy was easier than it really was.

The previous day's interviews in Redmond had gone well at first. But, as the hours passed and the interviews continued one after the other, exhaustion set in. The mastectomy, only weeks before, had robbed me of much of my stamina and physical strength. The surgery had exposed a vulnerability that I never allowed myself to acknowledge: my inability to do everything. The superwoman façade I had created was crumbling.

I had been a single mother longer than I had been married; that woman, the single mother, never got tired. She pulled it together to look after three children, cook dinner, work 45 to 60 hours a week, and still have energy to go out with friends on the weekend. I now realized that that woman no longer existed, and I was beginning to question whether I really wanted her back. Anyone in their right mind would have questioned my sanity for having come to Redmond for the interview; finally, I was beginning to question my sanity too.

Recalling my interview the day before, I remembered talking with the hiring manager and his supervisor. I liked them both; however, if I were looking for a reason not to be disappointed if the job was not offered to me, I found that reason during my final interview with the head of the department.

It was not her ramrod straight posture, her custom-fit blazer or her coiffed hair pulled tightly back into a bun that caused me to lose my efforts to maintain a positive state of mind; it was her invitation … "Tell me about yourself."

Her request was simple enough—perhaps meant to put me at ease and reveal my personality. Instead, it did the opposite. "Tell me about yourself" was a direct assault on my rapidly failing armor of deception. I was interviewing for a job a long way from home, trying to avoid the reality that the third messenger had brought me news of my impending death. Despite my hopeful optimism and positive outlook, in all likelihood, I wouldn't be alive long enough to add anything of lasting value to anyone I had met that day.

Her request exposed what I already knew. I was an imposter pretending that I was up to the task of working the long days that would be required of me and that I was hiding from the fact that, if what my mother had experienced was true for me, I would be dead before winter. In that moment, I could no longer circumvent the pain of my diagnosis by hiding behind work and accomplishments.

The woman with the perfectly coiffed hair and the straightforward request handed me what I wanted least–a mirror. Unexpectedly, long buried feelings of insignificance bubbled to the surface, exposing feelings of failed self-worth. I had walked into her office excited and confident; I walked out feeling disillusioned and dejected. Intrinsically, I sensed that no matter how good I was at my job or what I accomplished, it would never be good enough for her. Inherently, I knew that every word I spoke was being measured by a perfectionist with a deeply-rooted, critical spirit–my spirit recoiled. I knew that spirit all too well. I had grown up under its mantle, and it had taken residence in me.

I would never again see the woman who interviewed me that day, the woman behind the exquisite mask, the coiffed hair and the polite smile, but I would see her sisters again and again in lines at the grocery store and the airport, in restaurants and the workplace and in the place I wanted to see her least – I saw her in the mirror. We were, all of us, women whose feminine hearts had been betrayed and broken, doing our utmost to protect what was left of our feminine souls. We had succeeded in hiding our pain, but in the recesses of our being, masked behind degrees and accomplishments, empty smiles, manicured nails and mascara-laden lashes, we strove to perfect ourselves while hiding our sorrow and the anger we held for those who had betrayed us. In our sorrow and grief, we stood behind self-designed masks of sweetness and lies hoping that no one would see our scars.

Exhaustion had taken its toll on me. I could no longer pretend that my own efforts and hard work would get me what I wanted in life. Knowledge, self-sufficiency and possessions were not the answer either.

Everyone close to me had questioned my sanity for going to Redmond to interview for the job. I questioned it too, but felt something far greater than the interview had compelled me to go. Perhaps, just perhaps, God was redirecting my path.

Yet knowing how way leads on to way.
I doubted if I should ever come back.

Robert Frost

God is love and light. God's word is truth. Evil hates the light and it hates the truth

Susan Abar

9

Reflections of My Father

Reflections of My Father

Redmond, Washington
Saturday Morning, August 30, 2003

The sun danced golden through the hotel's balcony window welcoming autumn's arrival. I crawled out of the warm bed, opened the window and breathed in the fresh scent of cedars. Above me, towering pines reached out to touch the morning sky as the sun's rays sifted through their branches and the dew on the lawn shimmered to its light. Below me, rainbow-hued petunias nestled beside the red brick walkway, and I wondered how many hands had labored to create the gardens below.

Pushing thoughts about the previous day's interviews aside, memories of my father drifted into my consciousness. Long before I was born, my father had been stationed at Fort Lewis, Washington, not far from Redmond during World War II. My father had the dubious honor of being the first married man with a child from the state of Michigan to be drafted. Standing there I realized that my father had breathed in the same scent of cedars and watched the same golden sun as he waited for orders to be be deployed to the Pacific

Theater where the Japanese were still in the midst of fierce fighting even after Germany had surrender to Allied Forces.

Basking in the warmth of the early morning sun that chased away the dew, I understood, better than I ever wanted to understand, his emotions and the anguish he had to have felt as he surrendered to orders that could not be rescinded and prepared himself for a future over which he had no control. In all my years of growing up and raising children of my own, I had never once considered, until now, how my father had felt going off to war separated from his wife and his newborn daughter, my sister Lynne, by a war that he did not want to fight—a war from which he might not return.

My father did return from the war, some would say unscathed for he had no visible wounds, but that was not true. My father had not been assigned to a battlefield where men shot at one another; he had been assigned to a different battlefield, the military hospital in England where doctors and nurses fought to save the lives of wounded soldiers. My father's first assignment in the army was with the military police, but when the Army discovered he had been licensed as a barber in civilian life, they reassigned him to the hospital where he was required to cut the hair of men wounded in the war. He returned from war, his soul forever scarred by the sight of soldiers with severed limbs and rotting flesh…dying men whose bodies he was asked to help carry to the morgue to be prepared for burial when there was not enough help to do the job.

Every year on Memorial Day in the little town where I grew up, my father, respectfully quiet, stood on the sidewalk in front of Bobcean's Funeral Home and watched the procession of Veterans as they marched down the main street of town to the War Memorial to hear the names of brothers and sons...friends and neighbors...cousins and fathers called in remembrance. Those were precious days for me—days that endeared me to my father. Too young to understand the reason paunch-bellied men stuffed themselves into old uniforms pulled from their attics, I stood beside my father and watched as he came to attention when the drum corps marched past and the American flag hung at half mast. I followed his lead as he placed his right hand over his heart and reached down with his left to guide my little hand over my heart. Standing beside my father, I learned more about respect and pride, patriotism and sacrifice, than I ever learned anywhere else.

Even though my father was a Veteran, Dad never marched in the parades; I never knew why, but I had my own ideas. Walking behind the procession to the War Memorial, he stood reverently listening to the names of fallen heroes and with each name, a tear fell in silent salute to his friends— friends with whom he had gone to school and played football. And a tear for Bud, his best friend with whom he had been co-captain of their high school football team that won every game they ever played, except the game of war.

I clung to my father with my little arms wrapped around his leg for protection as rifle cracks echoed across the river honoring the men he had known in his youth—the boys, the young warriors, who on their way to becoming men were cut down in their prime. I knew the men who had died were honorable men because my dad was an honorable man. I would never know anything more about the men we honored each year or the pain of their loss forever embedded like shrapnel in Dad's ravaged heart. My dad's presence was my strength. His touch...my protection. And his silence... raw determination—the mask he used to hide his pain and grief.

The hotel where I stayed had been built with care so as not to destroy the trees and the foliage that surrounded it. Standing there soaking in the natural beauty of this place, I understood why my Dad said he would consider living in Washington if he ever moved from Michigan. Among the tall pines and hardwoods, memories of my Father surfaced effortlessly. As if it were yesterday, I could see him in his backyard tending his roses and mowing the grass. I remembered the smell of Old Spice as I stood on the floor board of the back seat and peeked over his shoulder as he pointed to a doe and her fawn grazing in a meadow filled with Queen Ann's Lace and golden-petaled Black-eyed Susans. I remembered how he cleared a patch of snow and spread bread crumbs for sparrows that had not escaped the harsh Michigan winters. And in my memories, I remembered the river behind Uncle Jim's house where we skated in the winter and fished in the summer. I tried not to remember the bad times that came later–the drunken rages, the foul words and the cutting comments that had assaulted my emerging femininity—but I couldn't entirely. My father...my protector, the first man I ever loved, left us, my family and me, the year I became a teenager.

He did not leave quickly; he left slowly–one bottle at a time. He took his wounds, the wounds of his heart, wounds he carried from his childhood and the war, wounds he never spoke about, still raw and bleeding, and hid himself from us. I was a young adult, still in my twenties, when my father stopped drinking. As an adult, I chose not to remember the verbally abusive father I had known as a teenager; instead, I chose to remember only the encouraging and loving father I had known as a child and the loving grandfather who carried my children, his grandchildren, in his arms.

When my father left his family to go to war, he boarded a train filled with men, who just like him, had been required to travel to a destination they had never seen. I had flown to Redmond on a plane filled with men and women not unlike myself, and like my father before me, I arrived at a destination unknown to me and to a destiny yet to be realized.

In the deepest recesses of my being, the pieces of the puzzle were coming together for me. I knew from the beginning that this trip to Pacific Northwest was one I had to take alone. I had not fully understood why I had refused Tina's offer to fly with me and help carry my bags when doctors had ordered me not to lift anything over five pounds. I was now beginning to understand at a level that I had not expected; I was on a journey to understand my soul's longing. This journey had a purpose much greater than the interview could offer; it gave me time to be alone and the opportunity to remember things that I had not been willing to remember.

I lingered in the memory of my father for a moment longer; then, turning back into the room I caught a glimpse of my reflection in the mirror. My father had been exceptionally handsome, but it had been an embarrassment for me as a little girl to be told that I looked like him and in the next breath be told how beautiful my mother was. In that moment, I looked at the reflection with a new curiosity. I could no longer refute what others had said. I had inherited everything I fought so hard to deny. There was no doubt; I was my father's daughter. I looked like him, and I thought like him. Like looking through a mirror dimly and then face-to-face, I saw the reflection of his blue eyes and his chiseled jaw. My eyes mimicked his, but my jaw was not chiseled and ruggedly handsome like his, it was feminine and softly defined.

In this place where no one could see me, I looked a little longer at the image in the mirror, amazed by what I saw, a beautiful woman... a woman I had not noticed before. Why had I not seen her? Why did I not know her? With all good intentions, I had misinterpreted my father's blessing. Yes, I, a woman did have a blessing from my father, but it was a blessing that I had not understood before. Far from home, driven by joblessness, cancer and certain death, gave me a different perspective on life. For the first time, I could see how wrong I had been and how harshly I had judged the woman in the mirror. I had not deserved the anger and the abuse that I had so willingly accepted from others and heaped upon myself.

My father's abuse had been verbal, and during my teens, I learned from my mother to acquiesce rather than risk an escalated confrontation with my father. My mother, wanting desperately to keep peace in the family, found it far easier to accept the inappropriate expression of my father's anger by either excusing his behavior as the way men behave or rescuing her children by soothing our feelings with the words, "he really didn't mean what he said." Mother's inability to confront the problem taught me that I too should acquiesce and do my best to avoid confrontation and not ruffle any feathers.

As a teen, I was impressionable and learned from watching the interactions of my parents that varying degrees of abuse could be expected. From that expectation, I managed to deduct that abuse was commonplace among men. Over the years, boundaries became blurred, and verbal abuse and emotional abuse escalated into physical abuse, first in one marriage and then a second. The final blow was my inability to thwart off the sexual assault by a man professing to be a friend of the family.

The men closest to me in my life had both unintentionally and purposefully betrayed. Sadly, they had taught me well. They taught me that I could not trust men emotionally or physically to be there when I needed them. They taught me that I could not depend upon them to protect me or my children.

Caught in a trap of dysfunction and flawed reasoning, I decided that being a woman was a source of weakness, and that men were the source of my problem. I came to the conclusion that if I was self-sufficient, I could be in control of my life. Determined to be financially secure, I left my teaching career and set out to prove to the world that I could do it all…including being head of household and providing a better life for both my children and me.

In the business world I put in the hours and worked hard. I felt safe in the corporate world around men. What I thought was a sense of camaraderie, a kinship with men in corporate America who like me were head of their households and worked hard to take care of their families was nothing of the sort. In the workplace, the lines were clear and the consequences defined. In the corporate world, I was comfortable around men because I had a back up. Federal laws protected me from harassment. My employee status as a female provided me with a hedge of protection and boundaries where I could be judged on my performance, a trade off for what I most feared, the essence of my soul – my femininity.

Just as the war had stolen my father's dreams, my dreams for a loving relationship had been stolen by a war with a different enemy. Just as my Dad had denied his feelings and had hidden his grief in a bottle, I had denied my feelings and had hidden my femininity behind a mask of self-sufficiency and determination. I was fearful of men who might hurt me. And I was afraid of my own femininity. I struggled to understand how meekness and strength could walk side-by-side and one not devour the other, and concluded that femininity was a weakness and masculinity was strength.

My father's hurt and brokenness had been passed on to me, and I had passed my hurt and brokenness on to my children. There was nothing left to do but forgive him and forgive myself. Like a healing balm, tears of forgiveness rolled down my cheeks, and I looked at the face in the mirror finally seeing the woman I had become – the woman inextricably intertwined with her father's story.

… when you call upon me and come and pray to me, I will hear you. "When you search for me, you will find me; if you seek me with all your heart. I will be found by you," declares the Lord …

Jeremiah 29:13-14

10

Surrender

Surrender

Redmond, Washington
Saturday Afternoon, August 30, 2003

It's amazing what we do to run from the truth. Still hiding the diagnosis of cancer from the people who had interviewed me, I accepted an invitation to meet with the company's realtor on Saturday, the day after the interview. The agent arrived promptly at 10:30 that morning, and together we traveled along winding black-topped roads from property to property looking for a place that was suitable for me.

At lunch time, we stopped at a quaint coffee shop for a cup of soup and a sandwich in Kirkland before traveling south along the western shore of Lake Washington to look at more properties. Several condos with a view of the lake piqued my interest, but one alone stood out. It was small and boxy—not particularly beautiful, but it had two features I could not resist: the price and the view. Built on a pier that jutted out over the lake, the 180 degree view of the north side of the lake was irresistible and convinced me that finding a way to make the cramped 675 square foot living space work would be well worth the effort.

Walking through the living area to the bedroom, I made mental notes. A couch with a hideaway bed would be perfect. It could provide a place to read in the day and a bed for visitors. The bedroom was small enough that only a double bed would fit comfortably. The closet was not much bigger than the 3' x 3' closet I knew as little girl, but the closet was a non-issue in the grand scheme of things. The company's dress code was business casual, so I really didn't need much in the way of clothes. The small kitchen with its compact, undersized appliances lined up against one wall reminded me of a sailboat's galley. Convinced this was the place I wanted to purchase, I asked the agent why the owner was selling. Her answer blindsided me...the owner had placed her condo on the market because she had Stage IV breast cancer. She was selling her possessions and moving out of her condo to move in with her daughter so that her daughter could care for her.

As I processed the agent's words, my eagerness to move from Texas and purchase the condo on Lake Washington suddenly dissipated like air escaping a punctured balloon. The reality was I had cancer, and if the doctors were correct, I was not going to be around long enough to warrant taking the job or moving to Washington. The similarity between the owner's situation and mine was uncanny. Where I placed my furniture and what color I painted the walls would not matter if I only had a short time left to live. Pretending that I had a future didn't guarantee me a future. Moving at this time would only further complicate my life – not just for me, but for everyone who cared about me.

It was nearly supper time when the realtor dropped me off at the hotel. I waited until her car pulled out of the parking lot before getting into the rental car. Retracing our morning drive to the small coffee shop where we had eaten earlier that day, I maneuvered into a parking space and dropped two quarters into the meter.

As I walked south along Lake Street toward Marsh Park, the brisk Pacific breeze whipped across the lake undeterred. In the distance, white jibs on sailboats billowed full - their sails as much a contrast to the deep blue waters of the Lake Washington as a match to the glistening white skyline of Seattle. I could no longer pretend that the cancer didn't exist just because I ignored its existence, nor could I pretend that getting a job would magically return some semblance of normalcy to my life. I was no longer in denial. The trip had been a journey of courage in the eyes of some, but in truth, it was the opposite. The trip had been a desperate attempt to run away from reality and deny my fear of death.

Pulling my jacket close around my neck to ward off the advancing chill in the wind, I listened to the sound of children and watched them play as they skipped rocks and ran from white-capped waves that threatened to soak their shoes. Not far away, their parents kept a protective watch over their young from an old wooden bench. With the next gust of wind, the children's mother leaned into her husband lovingly. Responding to her gentle nudge, he wrapped his arm around her shoulder and pulled her closer to him. The tenderness of their embrace tugged at my heart as the peals of their children's laughter brought back long forgotten memories of happier times, of soft, sandy beaches along Jamaica's North coast where my children and I had laughed and played in the warm Caribbean waters and listened to the melodic sounds of steel drums at sunset.

Jamaica had been my island home for ten years. Despite the difficulties I had experienced in the marriage to my children's father, I did have fond memories. I had traveled to the island as a young Peace Corps Volunteer and had fallen in love, not just with my children's father, but with the island and its people, its history and its traditions.

I loved the sunshine that permeated the Caribbean island with its steady temperatures and seasonal rains, and I cherished the panoramic view of Port Royal, Kingston and the cane fields of Clarendon from the balcony of our home at the top of Coopers Hill. I remembered the beauty of the magenta and orange bougainvillea against the stark white wall that separated our property and our neighbor's where our children played on their swing set shaded from the hot sun by the spreading branches of the almond tree with its thick leathery leaves. And I remembered the clatter of palm fronds in the wind along the crystal blue waters and white sand beaches of the Caribbean and the soothing sound of a steel band playing reggae and calypso under star-studded skies.

Looking across the deep blue waters of Lake Washington, those long forgotten memories surfaced as if it were only yesterday that I had watched my own children squealing with laughter as they buried their little toes in the warm sand and played in the shallow waters of the Caribbean Sea. It had been a time when I felt happy and sure that my marriage would last forever. How wrong I had been. Years later, my dreams of a loving and healthy marriage crumbled and beneath the rubble lay my shattered heart, a piece of my feminine soul, traumatized and bruised.

Still, as I watched the children play, I could not deny just how blessed my life had been. I had so many experiences that others never had. I had wonderful children and an extended family of friends and loved ones who cared about me. I had lived a full life. I was grateful. All that had seemed so wrong and so unfair disappeared as I realized that those who had wronged me had their own portion of betrayal and hurt, and I forgave them. I realized that over the years, I too, like them, had taken my betrayal and hurt and heaped it upon others.

The soothing rhythm of the waves upon the shore and the thought that these waters would be here long after I was gone comforted me. My children and the world would go on without me. I hoped that one day they would understand and forgive me for the wrongs that I had done to them. As the sun surrendered to the night, I surrendered my life to God.

I knew without a doubt that my life was part of God's exquisite plan, and that He had a plan for each of us. I knew that as imperfect as I was, He loved me. Whatever happened to me from this point forward was not in my hands, but in God's hands alone. My hope was in Him. It didn't matter which way the wind blew or whether I lived or died, nothing mattered now, except my relationship with God.

For forty years, I had wandered in the wilderness of pride and self-determination, a lonely desert of my own making. I had come to the conclusion that if I thought the right thoughts and did the right things, I held the secret to a good life, an easy life in my hands. I had been confident that I had the ability to do what needed to be done on my own. I had lived my life as if I had all the answers. In that moment, I knew the truth. Life wasn't about me and what I did; it was about being the person God created me to be and serving a God who, despite the chaos created by his erring people, was in control. Surrendering my life to God and his will, I renewed the promise that I had never fulfilled forty years before and committed my life to serve Him with whatever time I had left on earth. He had never abandoned me nor had He left me. While I strayed far from Him; He had always been there…watching and waiting for me to return to Him.

Surrendering to his will, I knew that everything would be all right. My life was no longer mine; it was His. In the face of death, God had given me peace. In surrender, He had given me hope. I had nothing to fear; my future was secure. Heaven waited and until my journey on earth was over, I had one purpose in my life and that was to serve Him and love those around me.

One-by-one the street lights came on. The winds died down and the waves subsided in the softening breath of the night. I knew I would never buy the condo or take the job in Redmond, even if it were offered to me. I walked back to the coffee shop, got into my car and drove back to the hotel. As darkness enveloped the earth, peace enveloped my soul. God's perfect plan was in place.

For I am the Lord, your God who takes hold of your right hand and says to you, "Do not fear; I will help you."

Isaiah 41:13

11

Going Home

Going Home

Redmond, Washington
Sunday, August 31, 2003

I woke Sunday morning refreshed and eager to get home, ready to embrace whatever the future held—afraid of nothing. I knew that I would never move to Redmond because I knew what I wanted: I wanted to go home. I wanted to be close to my family and friends.

Packing my suitcase, an audible sigh escaped my lips as I picked up the one remaining object from the dresser drawer. I stood there holding it, thinking how ridiculous it had been to take my bra, the most feminine garment in my possession and stuff it with athletic socks. The pretense was over. For three days, I had been involved in interviews answering questions and pretending that life would somehow return to normal if I landed a new job. I knew now that my life would never be the same again, and the truth was I didn't want it to be the same.

How little I understood about myself when I boarded the plane in Dallas that hot August morning to fly to the

Pacific Northwest. My trip to Redmond had not been about finding a job; it had been about something much bigger. It was part of my life's journey—a journey of surrender, an opportunity to heal old wounds and a time for discovering something I longed for and had lost touch with so many years before—my feminine heart. The journey had been about trusting in a God I could not see, the freedom that comes from forgiveness and letting go, and the joy of knowing how perfectly and wonderfully made I was in spite of myself, my choices and all that had happened in my life.

The cancer had robbed me of my breasts, but it had not stolen my femininity. Not unlike my father, who buried his losses in a bottle for years, I had hidden the song of my feminine heart in a job and accomplishments, behind a mask of pride and self-determination. My father's lost dreams of an education and becoming a doctor were interrupted by things that were out of his control: the death of his mother when he was only seven years old, the anger of his tormented father who committed suicide, the devastations of war and so much more that I would ever know about that had laid siege on his own heart.

My father's rages and the betrayal of two husbands were destructive to my feminine psyche, but it was the physical assault by the man who raped me that left me feeling ashamed that most threatened my sense of worth as a woman. To protect what was left, I put aside the longings of my feminine heart, the desire to be loved and cherished and bought into the rhetoric of women's lib attempting to prove my self-worth in a world that measured success in terms of achievement, education, status, and material possessions.

But those things never replaced my heart's longing to be cherished and honored nor did they replace my soul's need for intimacy and love.

In their place, I scaled walls and traveled more than one detour seeking fulfillment and praise from others for my performance by accumulating knowledge and degrees and working long hours. Because I was involved in Sunday School and my church, I thought I was doing the right things to earn God's approval, but now, I knew the truth. In all those years, I never understood what it meant to have a personal relationship with God, nor did I trust Him fully. I had been living by my own rules, the rules of a secular world that kept me from the most important and the most intimate relationship of all—my relationship with God.

The job lay-off and the breast cancer had been walls that had not prevented me from continuing to do things my own way; however, the diagnosis of the mass on my pancreas was a fence of thorns that I could not escape.

I carefully folded the bra and placed it in my suitcase; I had no need for a bra filled with athletic socks. Zipping my suitcase closed, I called the concierge. Within minutes, a light tap on the door announced the bellman's arrival. I opened the door and quietly stood back and watched as he picked up my bags with ease and placed them on the luggage cart. At one point in my life, carrying my own bags had been symbolic for me; it reinforced my sense of independence and my ability to take care of myself. I had adopted the notion that I didn't need any man in my life, let alone a man I could trust to take care of me.

I followed the bellman down the hallway to the elevator. No longer did I have to prove anything to anyone or do it all alone. I finally understood just how flawed my thinking had been and how difficult my thinking had made my life.

In the majesty of the Pacific Northwest beside Lake Washington, God had waited for me. Recommitting my life to Christ, God heard my cries of surrender, and I released my burdens to God. God's love and grace prevailed.

I drove to the airport captivated by the beauty of this world that I had been privileged to live in and comforted by God's grace. I whispered a prayer of thanks, grateful for rainbow-hued petunias and the velvet faces of jewel-colored pansies that I would never see again. I knew that God had His purpose for my life and His master plan was in place. If that plan was for me to die sooner rather than later, I could die in peace. I was going home.

But a poor widow came and put in two very small copper coins, worth only a fraction of a penny."

Mark 12:42

12

Two Pennies

Two Pennies

En route from Redmond, Washington to Dallas, Texas
Sunday, August 31, 2003

Leaving Redmond on Sunday morning, I drove to the airport with two thoughts on my mind: getting home and getting to my appointment with doctors at MD Anderson Cancer Center in Houston. After canceling the Whipple procedure with the surgeon in Dallas the week before my trip to Redmond, I followed the self-referral process at MD Anderson and set up an appointment with an oncologist who specialized in pancreatic cancer. Afterward, I called everyone I knew to let them know about the diagnosis. Aunt Winnie's daughter, Winnie Jean had been one of my girlfriends in high school. We both left Michigan after college, and Winnie had ended up working at Baylor College of Medicine in Houston. When I called her, I never expected to learn that Winnie personally knew one of the doctors leading an important research project for Dr. James Abbruzzese, a leading expert in pancreatic cancer, the same doctor that I was scheduled to see on Tuesday, September 2nd, only two days away.

Following the signs near the airport to the drop off the rental car, I drove into the parking garage and up the ramp to the third floor. Eager to get to the terminal as quickly as possible, I checked the mileage, opened the trunk from inside the car and got out to get my luggage. Determined not to cause injury to my body that was still healing from the mastectomy, I used leverage rather than brute strength to slide the luggage to the floor of the parking garage. I walked around the car and checked each section to make sure there were no dings on the doors and no scratches to the paint. Waiting for the customer service representative who was with another customer, I looked around at other customers scurrying to get their luggage when I happened to look down at the pavement. Inches from the toe of my shoe was an old copper penny that had fallen out of someone's pocket. The words from a nursery rhyme my mother used to say came to mind.

> *See a penny pick it up,*
> *All day long you'll have good luck.*
> *Put a penny in your shoe*
> *So good luck will follow you.*

Sheepishly, I looked around to make sure no one was watching. Before kneeling down, I hesitated momentarily and looked heavenward. Honoring my commitment and my promise to trust God for everything, I looked up and whispered, "I'm really not superstitious; I'm trusting in You." Picking up the penny, I slid the penny into my right shoe. Handing the customer service representative my mileage, I grabbed my luggage and headed for the terminal.

The lines of people waiting to go through security were longer and slower than normal. Joining the shoulder to shoulder crowd, I lined up with other passengers and wondered if I would get through security in time to make my flight. As the growing number of passengers funneled into the single file line to have their belongings checked and scanned, I felt a growing concern. I had things to accomplish over the course of the next two days, and time was running out. If I missed the plane it would impact my ability to get ready for my Tuesday appointment at MD Anderson only two days away.

Remembering the penny, I slipped off my right shoe and looked. It was there where I put it—smack dab in the middle of the arch of my shoe. Sliding my foot back into my shoe, I looked up again and smiled as if God and I had a special secret of our own. Little did I know at the time that God had a surprise in store for me. The truth was...I had no clue as to how significant the secret really was. It would take months for me to understand the true significance of the penny.

Getting through security, I gathered my things as quickly as I could, slipped my shoes back on and headed to my gate as quickly as possible. Without a minute to spare, I scrambled to my seat and fastened my seat belt. Moments later, as the plane leveled off, I gazed out the window grateful to be alive and for the chance to see the majestic sight of snow-capped Mount Rainier once more. I breathed a silent prayer of thanks grateful to be going home and at peace with my past...at peace with my future.

Changing planes in Denver for the second leg of my journey home, I quickly found my seat next to the aisle and started to settle in. Slipping off my shoes for comfort, I remembered the penny. Not finding it in my right shoe, I looked in the left. The penny wasn't in either shoe. Coming to the conclusion that the coin had been lost in my haste to get through security at the airport, I slid my feet back into my shoes. Disappointed that I didn't see the penny, I got up and walked to the rear of the plane to stretch, still comforted by the new found peace I experienced in surrendering to God and the knowledge that life was not about trusting good luck or pennies.

The plane had no more than twenty passengers and the royal blue carpet that stretched from one end of the cabin to the other looked brand new. The saddle brown leather that wrapped around the empty, passenger seats was still stiff and new. Taking my time to return to my seat, I noticed a glint of copper in the middle of the aisle ahead of me. As if measured and deliberately placed, heads up in my path—I realized it was a penny. Not a soul was sitting near me. I assumed what I thought was obvious; the penny, in all likelihood, must have fallen out of my shoe and rolled into the middle of the aisle. I kneeled down for the second time that day to pick up the penny. As I turned the penny over in the palm of my hand, I thought it odd that I hadn't noticed the penny earlier when I walked to the back of the plane. Determined not to lose the penny a second time, I slipped it into my left shoe this time. Once again I smiled, looked heavenward and whispered quietly, "Lord, I'm trusting in you."

The rest of the trip was uneventful. I arrived home eager to unpack and get ready for the trip to Houston on Monday. My appointment to go to MD Anderson had been confirmed for Tuesday, September 2. I had 24 hours to get ready for the most defining journey of my life.

When I arrived home, I checked in with my daughters, Bridget and Kirsty, and my son's fiancee, Angie. She had good news; Aubrey would be home for two weeks sometime that fall. The thought thrilled me. I wanted to give him a hug and tell him one more time how much I loved him and how proud I was of him. Time was short and the chance of ever celebrating another birthday or Christmas holiday was unlikely

I emptied my luggage, separated the dark clothes from the light and threw a load of laundry into the washer. Ready to relax and enjoy the rest of the evening in the comfort of my own home, I slipped off my shoes. Looking inside my shoes for the penny, I stopped and looked again. There in the bottom of each shoe was a penny: one in my right and one in my left. Fishing out the pennies, I placed them in the palm of my hand. Turning them over, I studied each one in the hope that a date on one of the coins might carry some significance—like the year of one of my children's birth or an anniversary, but there was none. Wondering how in the world I had ended up with two pennies, I tucked both pennies into the jewelry box on my dresser still puzzled by the appearance of those two little coins.

I recalled the story of Jesus in Mark 12:42 when He pointed out to His disciples a poor widow who sacrificed more than the wealthy when she gave "two small copper coins worth less than a penny." Jesus understood how much those two small coins meant to the widow. He understood her sacrifice.

He also understood the worth of a woman whose feminine heart had been betrayed and buried, a woman whose life's circumstances had encouraged her to believe she was worth less than she was. I was that woman. The most important men in my life, my father and both husbands, had (both unintentionally and intentionally) left me feeling unworthy and broken. Overtime, I began to believe that I was the cause of my father's anger and my husbands' betrayals and unfaithfulness. I knew better, but deep inside I blamed my inability to be a better daughter and more perfect wife for their failings. And I internalized the belief that women whose marriages had survived were somehow superior to me. Because of not one, but two failed marriages, I concluded subconsciously that I was less worthy than others.

Surrendering my life to Christ on the shores of Lake Washington, I laid my burdens at the foot of the cross and knew that my sins, everything I had ever done wrong in my life, were forgiven. My slate was clean, and my life restored. No longer burdened by the wounds that others had inflicted on me or the wounds I inflicted on myself, I was free to be the woman God intended me to be. Trusting in God meant I no longer had to worry about anything. God was in control and my relationship with Him brought me peace of mind. God had allowed me to find two insignificant pennies and put them in my shoes, so that I would never forget that the foundation of my faith on which I stand is grounded in trusting in God for everything. It took me months to realize that on those two small copper coins that I had slipped into my shoes were the words—In God We Trust.

Whenever the rainbow appears in the clouds, I will see it and remember the everlasting covenant between God and all living creatures of every kind on the earth." So God said to Noah," This is a sign of the covenant I have established between me and all life on the earth."

Genesis 9:16-17

13

The Midst of the Storm

In the Midst of the Storm

En route from Dallas to Houston, Texas
Monday, September 1, 2003

I loaded the Explorer and headed for Houston much later on Monday afternoon than I intended. Amid the flurry of emotions I was feeling, I felt a need to not put off anything that in the past I might have let slide before a long trip. The difference from past trips I had taken was that I didn't know when or if I would return. Making sure the bills had been paid, I took time to change the sheets and make sure everything was in its place. I reasoned that if doctors in Houston made the decision to perform surgery, I would have a clean house and fresh sheets to come home to; but if I didn't return, I knew my children would need a place to stay after the funeral and memorial service in order to go through my personal effects. Making sure everything was in order had taken more time than I expected.

Harriet and Jack were expecting me. I would be staying with them at their house in the Woodlands about an hour north of Houston. Looking forward to seeing them, I thought about our traditional get together for the Dickens

Festival in Galveston. Dressing up in period costumes reflecting the late 1800s, we had over the course of the past several years kicked off our Christmas Holidays by going to Dickens in the Strand the first weekend of every December. For the occasion, Harriet and I had both purchased hats that completed our costumes and made us feel very eloquent. Harriet had purchased a black bonnet with a gray and white ostrich feather that matched her black cape. A ribbon tied under her chin kept her hat securely where it belonged when wind gusts off the Gulf of Mexico swept through the Strand. Quite different from Harriet's hat, my hat looked a bit more like an upside-down platter trimmed with two inch ruffles. Totally ignorant of wind gusts, I had purchased my hat because the huge purple ostrich feather matched my purple cape. When the gust of wind off the Gulf hit my hat the first time, it immediately flew off my head and rolled down the Street like a runaway saucer. From that moment on, I was a bit more careful to pay more attention to the wind than I had before. Jack, very much a part of the festivities, had his own Dickens on the Strand wardrobe. Not about to be outdone by either Harriet or me, Jack's gray mourning suit complete with tails, white spats, cane and gray top hat landed him the job of escort to the two of us.

Going to Galveston to celebrate Christmas was a fun time for the three of us. Street vendors sold their Christmas wares while jugglers and carolers entertained the crowds. Setting aside any pretense of healthy eating that one weekend, we allowed ourselves caramel apples and funnel cakes, turkey legs and kettle corn. At the end of the day, as the Queens Parade passed and Scrooge with Tiny Tim on his shoulders wished everyone a Merry Christmas, we promised to keep the tradition going and return the following year.

This year was different. Harriet and Jack were not welcoming me to their house for a casual visit or to dress up for Dickens on the Strand. Once they knew of the doctor's report and that I had an appointment at MD Anderson, they invited me to stay with them. Committed to our friendship, Harriet arranged to be out of her office so that she could be with me during my doctor appointments. If needed, she was prepared to arrange her schedule to be with me during surgery or if my illness required...hospice.

Heading south out of Dallas on I-45 that Monday afternoon, the road between Dallas and Huntsville was clear, and I made good time over the course of the first two hours. For several days a huge tropical depression had been brewing in the Gulf of Mexico. My first warning that the storm had made landfall and was sweeping inland was the sight of ominous black clouds in the distance as I approached Madisonville, Texas. Staying on course, the storm and I collided in Huntsville. As the wind picked up and sheets of rain pounded my vehicle turning the highway into a shallow river and reducing visibility to near zero, drivers pulled to the side of the road and parked their cars under overpasses and in nearby parking lots to wait out the storm. I was not one of them; neither was the driver in front of me, who, despite reducing her speed dramatically, suddenly lost control of her car and hydroplaned off the road avoiding a near collision with another car by the skin of her teeth.

The intensity of the storm increased with each mile, and I thought about Tina and her offer to travel to Houston with me as she had offered to travel with me to Redmond. This time I refused her offer, not because I didn't want the companionship, but because I needed quiet time to think— time alone with God.

Rain thudding against the metal shell that protected me from the elements drowned out my ability to hear and wiped out my ability to see what lay in front of me much beyond my headlights. I called Harriet to tell her that I would be late. In the background, Jack suggested I pull off the road and wait until the storm passed.

Gripping the steering wheel even tighter, I ignored his advice and continued on my way in midst of the storm despite sheets of rain that slowed my progress to a crawl. My need to be in control usurped common sense. Driving through the last curtain of rain as the sun drifted beneath the western horizon turning velvet gray skies into night. I understood more clearly the term free will. I had surrendered my life to God, but not my will. I had made this trip alone so that I could focus on God. But when the storm hit, my focus was on the storm and driving through it; it was not on God. Jack's suggestion was a wise one that I discounted in my determination to get to my destination. How many times had God tried to get my attention, and I had ignored Him the way I ignored Jack?

As the setting sun slipped beneath the treetops, I looked to the east and saw the faintest remnant of a rainbow. It was short. It was wide. And it was barely visible against the darkening sky of night, but it was a rainbow. And it reminded me that there were other ways of handling life's storms than just charging through them. Noah had listened to God and had survived the flood when others had not heeded God's warning. After the flood was over, God placed a rainbow in the sky as "an everlasting covenant between God and all living creatures…"

It was dark and the porch light was on by the time I arrived at Harriet and Jack's that evening. They greeted me with open arms, and Jack carried my luggage to their guest room on the second floor. That night, as I curled up in bed and reflected on the day, I smiled…grateful for God's presence in the midst of life's storms, a rainbow and friends who cared enough to help shoulder my burden.

"... The Lord is full of compassion and mercy."

James 5:11

A Woman Named Mercy

A Woman Called Mercy

Houston, Texas
Tuesday, September 2, 2003

Long before sunrise, I woke to the soft clunk of coffee mugs being pulled from the cupboard and the aroma of freshly brewed coffee wafted up the stairs. Moments later, the sound of footsteps in the hallway outside my bedroom door preceded Harriet's quiet knock checking to see if I was up. Dressing quickly, I placed the medical records I brought with me from Plano into my computer bag and headed for the kitchen where Harriet and Jack waited for me.

An hour's drive to downtown Houston, my appointment at MD Anderson required that I be there by seven that morning. Jack took my computer bag from me, rolled it out to the driveway and placed it in the trunk of Harriet's car. One step ahead of Houston's notorious humidity and rush-hour traffic, we arrived at the cancer center and registered at admissions with time to spare. Heading to my first appointment, Harriet led the way, guiding me through a maze of unfamiliar hallways and elevators to the desk at the Gastrointestinal Center on the seventh floor. Checking in with the receptionist and following protocol, an assistant took my weight and blood pressure before handing the results to the nurse. Confirming my name and ID numbers, the nurse asked for my medical records. I fished the cumbersome folders out of the computer bag and handed them over to her before she directed us to a small room to wait for the doctor.

The next person we met was the Physician's Assistant, the PA. Introducing herself to us, she explained that she would be entering data about my medical history on the computer, and that the doctor would be in as soon as he and his team had completed reviewing the medical records and films that I had carried with from the hospital and the doctor's office in Plano.

When she was finished asking questions, the PA made a general inquiry, "How are you doing?" Purposely avoiding any reference to the mass, I told her about the job interview that I had just returned from and my hopes for the future and the possibility that I might be moving to the Pacific Northwest. I made reference to the cancer by commenting about my plans to get chemotherapy in Washington if needed.

She became extraordinarily quiet and stood there looking at me, a bit mystified by my response. Intuitively, I knew what she was thinking. She was thinking that I was either in denial and deceiving myself or I didn't understand the seriousness of the mass on my pancreas. The silence grew longer as she considered what to say and how to say it. As caring and compassionate as she tried to be, the only words I remembered were, "The doctors are looking at your scans. You need to be prepared to go home and surround yourself with friends and family."

Before leaving the room, she hesitated and inquired if I was okay. I nodded with my head to the affirmative— neither wanting nor able to process everything she said. As she closed the door, I looked at Harriet. Harriet's eyes confirmed more than I wanted to know. I had heard the PA correctly. She was right and I knew it. Letting out a deep sigh, I knew that there was only one thing left that I could do. I bowed my head and prayed.

Moments later, the doctor entered the room. Making us comfortable in his presence, he introduced himself and sat down on a metal stool. Dr. Abbruzzese was slender and tall. In his starched white coat he looked professional and exuded the confidence of a knowledgeable, well-trained medical professional. I felt confident that I was in the best of hands. His demeanor and carefully chosen words exuded a quiet strength. Speaking simply and factually, he explained that the reports and the scans that I brought with me revealed a mass in the head of the pancreas known as the uncinate process. He went on to explain that treatment was not an option, nor was surgery. There was nothing more they could do. The only other thing the doctor could provide me with that offered any kind of consolation was an opportunity to participate in a research study related to pancreatic cancer that he and his department were involved in.

I remembered my mother's words when she asked the doctor at the University of Michigan if there was a study that she could participate in "...whatever I can do for my family and my grandchildren, I'll do." She didn't want anyone else to experience the disease that she and her father had contracted. I understood her words. I wanted to make a difference in the lives of my children and others. If this was the only opportunity I had left in my life, I wanted to participate.

The study required that the researchers start from scratch and redo all the scans and blood work to create a new baseline using only MD Anderson's staff and equipment. I met with the social workers and signed the paperwork giving the hospital and the university permission to use the results for research. They informed me that the diagnostic tests would take the entire day. The first test was scheduled to begin during the second half of the morning and end around dinner time. Dr. Abbruzzese assured me that they could have the results for me the following afternoon. Gathering up the paperwork and putting it in my computer bag with the rest of my medical papers, Harriet and I walked over to the radiology department to prepare for the first set of tests.

It was late when we walked to the second floor for the last set of tests. Halls and waiting rooms that bustled with activity only an hour before seemed strangely void of people. Surveying the room, I took my seat as another phlebotomist walked her last patient to the door before excusing herself to go home. Long past dinner time, chairs once filled with patients were empty now. It felt strange to be one of the last two people in the lab—stranger still, to be the last patient. Calmly, the woman who read my lab orders turned to inform me that there was an issue. The lab orders were accurate, but the authorizing signature to conduct the blood work was missing. Concerned that obtaining the authorization from the doctor that late in the evening might require more time than I had planned for, she asked courteously, "Do you have time to wait?"

I thought about Harriet waiting patiently with me throughout the day and knew that she would be okay. Knowing that time was the only thing I had left that was worth anything to me, I answered, "I have the rest of my life." It was long past supper time when she received the approval.

Putting on her gloves with care, I felt a tenderness in her touch as she tied the tourniquet around my arm and gently massaged my vein. To avoid looking at the needle as she drew blood from arm, I looked up at her face. It was at that moment that I saw her eyes. They were beautiful beyond description, and something about them captivated me. Interrupting my thoughts of her, a sudden surge of emotion washed over me. Blanketed by an unexplainable swell of shame, I lowered my head in embarrassment and looked down at the floor. Yearning to see her eyes again, I tried to look up, but a heaviness thwarted my efforts. Only when she turned away and focused on the vials of my blood did I dare to look up again. I sat there in awe, wondering what had just happened.

The soft ring of the technician's phone interrupted her concentration, and I overheard her barely audible words, "I'll be home soon…" Her words reminded me of the words I had too often spoken to my children when they called me at the office and asked me when I was coming home. Overhearing only bits of her conversation, I felt a touch of sadness that she too, for reasons of her own, had chosen to take time away from her family to stay late and to look after my needs, when she should have been home with her family. Feeling like a kindred spirit, I wanted to tell her that the blood she drew from my veins would replenish itself, but the time she spent away from her family could never be replaced. I thought about the hours I had spent as a teacher grading papers after school and the hours I had spent in the corporate arena completing projects late into the evening thinking I was benefiting my career and thus, my children. I knew now that it was all an illusion.

The diagnosis of the mass had made me acutely aware of time...how little time I had left and how much time I had misused. I realized that those hours that I had spent working late were hours of togetherness and memories that I had stolen from my children. Unlike a bank account that can be replenished, there is no time account to which we can save hours and minutes to be withdrawn at a later time. I could not withdraw an hour to go to my son's wrestling match that I had missed nor could I save time for the future to play with grandchildren yet to be born. I realized the old adage there's always tomorrow was a lie. Tomorrow never comes. Today, this hour, this minute is all we have.

Yet there she was, a perfect stranger, a woman who had refused another technician's offer to take my case so that she could go home on time. The phlebotomist's words to the other technician were straightforward and effortless, "I'll take care of her. She's my patient." Grateful for her time, I looked up at her and said, "I want to say thank you." With eyes glued to the task before her, she nodded her head acknowledging that she had heard me. The nonverbal nod of her head spoke louder than words. I knew that she really did not understand how much I appreciated her staying late. How could she? She had little idea of what I was thinking.

A second time, I looked at her. Still busy and as focused on her work as ever, I said, "I want to say thank you to you." And a second time without looking up from her task or making eye contact, she nodded in acknowledgement. I was disappointed by her response for two reasons: first, because I wanted to see her eyes again and second, because I knew that if it were not for me sitting in that chair, the last patient in her lab, she could be on her way home. She could have passed me on to another phlebotomist when the shift changed, but she had not; she had chosen to see me through the lab work. I hesitated and thought through what might get her to stop what she was doing and look up for just a moment. Collecting my thoughts, I was determined to get her attention—whatever it took. I turned to her one last time. Patiently and deliberately, I said, "I want to say thank you to you. What is your name?" And like the whisper of an angel's wing she answered, "Mercy."

In this tiny room with no windows, where time slipped away, Mercy spoke her name and gave me more than I ever asked for. I sat there stunned…awestruck…unable to speak. I knew the moment she spoke her name that her response was not a coincidence and her presence was not an accident; God had orchestrated it all.

In the midst of the most difficult time of my life… under circumstances over which I had no control, a sense of peace washed through me and like a gentle wave upon the sand erasing the faintest footprint upon the shore, my fears evaporated.

God, all knowing, had placed a woman named Mercy in my path to reassure me that He was with me. And I knew without a doubt that His plans for me were in place. He knew my grief and had heard the cry of my heart and in His way, He answered. I knew beyond a shadow of a doubt that God was in control. And with God in control, there was nothing that I needed to be afraid of...not even death.

> *I love the Lord, for He heard my voice;*
> *He heard my cry for mercy.*
> > *Psalms 116: 1*

"For I know what I have planned for you," says the Lord. I have plans to prosper you not to harm you. I have plans to give you a future filled with hope."

Jeremiah 29:11

15

Hope and a Future

Hope and a Future

Houston, Texas
Wednesday, September 3, 2003

The physicians and staff at MD Anderson Cancer Center were kind, but they didn't mince words that might have confused me or pretend that everything was going to be all right. The doctors at MD Anderson agreed with the findings of the first radiologist in Plano who wrote that the scans revealed "…a well circumscribed 1.5 cm low density lesion in or adjacent to the uncinate process of the pancreas [that was] suspicious for a cystic pancreatic neoplasm." A neoplasm is an abnormal mass of tissue that is created when cells divide more than the should or don't die when they should. The abnormal mass is called a tumor. The doctors at MD Anderson reviewed the second set of scans as well and concurred with the second radiologist that the second set of scans performed in Plano did reveal a lesion that had grown significantly to "2 cm in diameter" in only five days and was "… likely a second primary necrotic node…" Three teams of doctors had reviewed my scans, and their conclusions were the same. I could no longer hope that one of the medical professionals had made an error or misread my scans. Since chemo treatment and surgery was not a viable option, there was little hope.

Meeting Mercy was a turning point. I knew that God had placed her in my life for a reason. When Harriet and I left the hospital late that evening, I experience a deep, inexplicable sense of peace. No longer in denial, no longer refuting the diagnosis, I finally acknowledged that the doctors did not have a solution. I began to wonder less about death and more about what I could do to help prepare my children for the inevitable. I wondered how my children would handle my death and my absence from their lives. I wanted my son home from Iraq as soon as possible. And I wanted my last moments to be loving and without drama—not for me, but for my children.

Harriet and I returned to MD Anderson the next afternoon on Wednesday, September 3, 2003 to learn the results of the previous day's tests from Dr. Abbruzzese. Fifteen minutes early for my appointment, Harriet and I walked up to the receptionist's desk of the gastroenterology clinic, and I gave the receptionist my name. The receptionist looked up at me and seemed to blurt out as if I had done something terribly wrong, "Where have you been?"

Surprised by what seemed to me to be an accusation that I was late, I felt the need to defend myself and started to respond that I was early. Interrupting before I could finish, her body language displayed an urgency that was uncharacteristic of MD Anderson employees. Abruptly, she said, "The doctors have been waiting for you ...". Turning to the other receptionist and asking her to handle things until she returned, she stood up and walked around to the visitor's side of the desk. Clearly on a mission, she looked at Harriet, the computer bag and then at me in an effort to size up the situation as quickly as she could. Using fewer words and more action, she made an executive decision and grabbed my computer bag entreating us to follow. Harriet and I looked at each other. Puzzled by urgency and tone of the receptionist's request, we followed in submission.

Barely a month out of surgery, emotionally and physically drained, keeping pace with the receptionist was a bit of a challenge. Harriet heard my winded breathing and checked to make sure I was okay. Turning to walk through one last set of doors into a long hallway, the clicking heels of the receptionist's shoes against the linoleum floor seemed to increase in volume as the pace of her steps slowed. Leading us down a long, windowless corridor, my eyes fixed on an open door on our left. As each step brought us nearer to the room, the sound of voices coming from within grew curiously silent. A team of doctors wearing starched white lab coats looked up as I looked in. One-by-one, our eyes met as each expressionless face turned toward me. The last pair of eyes belonged to Dr. Abbruzzese, the oncologist with whom I had spoken the day before. At the sight of him, my knees weakened, and my heart grew heavy. Now I understood the woman's urgency; the doctors were waiting for me.

Slowing to a full stop beside a dark doorway, the receptionist stepped inside and turned on the light revealing a room painted in shades of gray with the barest furnishings. Our escort directed us to take our seats in the consulting room and to wait for Dr. Abbruzzese. Harriet and I sat down as directed and looked at each other wide-eyed...afraid to speak. The receptionist's demeanor as she led us through the hallways had alarmed me, but seeing the doctors as they looked up at me as we passed the room terrified me. Our wait was not long. Minutes later, Dr. Abbruzzese knocked softly, opened the door and entered. He acknowledged us with a silent nod and hesitated before speaking. My body trembling in fear was ready for the worst. Without a hint of what he was about to say, the doctor spoke then concluded with the last words I ever expected to hear, "There is no mass."

I sat there in utter disbelief...unable to understand. Prepared for the worst, I was not prepared for the best news of all. In Dallas, I had had two sets of scans on two separate days. Experienced doctors, experts in their field, had consulted with one another and had agreed that the scans revealed a "fast-growing mass".

I knew I should be leaping and shouting for joy, but I couldn't. The good news contradicted all reason...everything the medical professionals had prepared me for...everything I was prepared for. Apprehensive to respond with any emotion, but the most rational thought, I sat there looking at him, bewildered by his words, words that contradicted everything I was expected to hear. I was afraid to speak. I wondered if their reports were accurate. Could it be possible that they, the best doctors in the world, had misread the results? I was afraid to trust him, afraid that in the next breath, seemingly good news would be countered and hope would be snatched from me.

Overwhelmed and unsure of what or who to believe, I finally asked, "How is that possible?" The doctor shook his head ever-so-slightly, raised his shoulders with a slight shrug and responded that he didn't know. As far as I was concerned, the doctors didn't have to know what had happened. I knew. It was God. And God had performed a miracle. It would take time for me to process the doctor's words and the magnitude of God's gift.

I had prayed for healing and believed it could happen, but I never knew anyone who had had such an experience, such an answer to prayer. The mere thought that God would give someone like me a miracle that would save me from death was incomprehensible. I was an imperfect woman who had my own list of wrong doings. I was not a horrible person, but I had had my backsliding days and over the years had amassed my own personal collection of sins, significant enough that I couldn't imagine that God would choose to give me a miracle–but He had.

Harriet and I left the hospital amazed by God's mercy and my encounter with a woman called Mercy the day before. That night, I fell asleep knowing that I had been protected by a loving God who was capable of anything.

The next morning, as Jack loaded my luggage into the back of my old Explorer, I hugged Harriet good-by and thanked both of them for all they had done for me. Still in awe and wonder, I backed the car into the street, straightened the wheel and headed home to Plano. During the drive home, I called everyone who knew about the mass, and reported the good news. Reaching my oncologist, Dr. Stokoe was delighted for me, but cautiously optimistic. He recommended that I come in the following Thursday to start chemotherapy as soon as possible. I still had one more battle ahead of me, my battle with breast cancer.

I love the Lord, for He heard my voice;
He heard my cry for mercy.
Because He turned his ear to me,
I will call on Him as long as I live.
The cords of death entangled me,
The anguish of the grave came upon me;
I was overcome by trouble and sorrow.
Then I called on the name of the Lord:
'O Lord, save me!"
The Lord is gracious and righteous;
Our God is full of compassion.
The Lord protects the simple hearted;
When I was in great need, He saved me.
Be at rest once more, O my soul,
For the Lord has been good to you.
For you, O Lord, have delivered my soul from death.

Psalms 116: 1-8

*You turned my wailing into dancing;
You removed my sack cloth and clothed
me with joy, That my heart may sing to
You and not be silent. O Lord my God,
I will give You thanks forever.*

Psalms 30: 11-12

16

Bald, Bold and Beautiful

Bald, Bold and Beautiful

Plano, Texas
October 2003

Making an appointment to meet with my oncologist in Plano when I arrived home, Dr. Stokoe greeted me with an ear to ear smile and held out his arms to offer a hug when I walked into his office. He had known my story. He knew about the layoff, the breast cancer, the diagnosis of the mass, the job interview, and now—the miracle. He was as thrilled for me about the report from MD Anderson as I was. Now focused on the reason I was in his office, we scheduled my chemotherapy to begin treatment for the breast cancer the following week.

My daughter Bridget flew in from New York City and sat with me as the oncology nurse introduced the first round of the red-colored concoction, the Adriamycin and Cytoxan, into my veins. Other than a metallic taste in my mouth, I felt fine when we left the oncology center after the chemotherapy.

That afternoon, Bridget drove me home, and I resisted her efforts to tuck me into bed and treat me as if I were sick.

Later that night, as my body violently rejected the intrusion of chemicals and the nausea racked my body, I welcomed her efforts to wash my face with a warm wash cloth and wrap me in a soft blanket. All night long my daughter lay at the foot of my bed, listening and checking on me to make sure I was okay. Too weak to care for myself, I realized that the days when she was a child and I was her caretaker were, for the moment, reversed. That night my youngest took care of me in my time of need—a subtle realization that parents taking care of their children when the children are young, and adult children taking care of their parents as their parents aged was part of God's master plan.

The next morning, Bridget called Dr. Stokoe to report the severity of my reaction to the chemo. He ordered a prescription for Neulasta®, a drug that reduced my nausea and helped raise my red blood cell count supporting my body's efforts to heal. My body's reaction to the chemo opened my eyes to the fact that chemotherapy was a far bigger challenge than I had thought it was going to be. Experiencing first hand the stress of the chemo on my body, I realized just how naive and foolish I was for having even the faintest thought that I could move to a new city, start a new job, begin chemo treatments, and still be an effective employee. The facts were on the table. I now knew that if I had landed the job in Redmond, I would have been a highly ineffective employee. God knew what He was doing when He allowed me to go to Redmond, and He knew what He was doing when He didn't open the door for me to get the job. When my strength returned, Bridget returned to New York, and the girls from the Welcome Class at church took turns looking after me.

I knew that my medical bills that I had not yet seen were mounting. In moments of quiet, I did my best to turn my worries over to God and asked for His guidance. Over the course of several days I felt a persistent nudging in my spirit to contact Larry, my former manager. When I mentioned to my closest friends that I was considering contacting him they discouraged me, sure that I was setting myself up for rejection. There was something in my spirit that would not let the thought go. I felt emboldened knowing I had nothing to lose. Despite their objections, I picked up the phone the week following my first chemo session in hopes that I could get an appointment with him before my hair started falling out. It was a pride thing; I didn't want Larry to have pity on me because I was going through chemo. I wanted him to consider me on my merits and allow me to work on a contract basis if he had any special projects. His secretary made the appointment for the following Tuesday.

The morning of my appointment with Larry, I did my best to style my new hairdo that my hairdresser had cut only the day before. Looking in the mirror, I noticed a few strands of hair were already starting to fall out. According to the information I had, I could expect my hair to be completely gone by the third week. I was in the middle of week two. Walking into the familiar lobby of the building I had worked in for four years, I wondered if my friends had been right, and that I was not only going to be disappointed, but also embarrassed by my decision to speak with Larry. Melanie, the receptionist on duty, who I knew quite well, greeted me warmly. Not knowing about the cancer, she complimented me on my new hairdo. Chatting for a moment, Melanie reached in her purse and pulled out a folded strip of paper. Stepping out from behind the desk, she gave me a warm hug and handed it to me. Unfolding the paper, I read these words:

> *For I know the plans I have for you says the Lord, plans to prosper you and not to harm you, plans for a future filled with hope.*
>
> *Jeremiah 29:11*

I stood there looking at the paper and looking at her. She had no idea what she had done. God was at work again. For me it was clear, God used Melanie to give me a message of encouragement and hope. As I thanked her, the lobby door opened. It was Larry's secretary inviting me to follow her.

Larry hadn't changed at all in the four months since I had last seen him. Welcoming me to his office as he had done many times before, I sat down and shared with him all that had happened. I asked him if he would consider hiring me as a consultant if any contract work became available. Four days later, the man, who had been my first messenger took on a new role, the role of Good Samaritan, carrying the news that the company was reinstating my employment. My job ended on December 31, 2003, the day after my last surgery, a month after my final chemo treatment.

I learned many important lessons that day. I learned that I needed to pay closer attention to Proverbs 3:5 that said "Trust in the Lord with all your heart and lean not on your own understanding." I needed to trust in the nudging in my spirit, the still small voice of God directing my path. And I learned that if I was going to follow God, I had to set aside my pride, my fear of rejection and step out of my comfort zone and be bold when God emboldened my spirit.

I was reminded that God does not work in ways that I understood and expected. He placed Melanie in my path with a hug and a small folded strip of paper with a scripture from Jeremiah 29:11 to encourage me and give me hope. And God had appointed Larry to be my first messenger, the bearer of news that my job, my livelihood, was being taken from me. And God, in His wisdom placed Larry in a position to rehire me and be my Good Samaritan.

In Luke 10:29, Jesus told the story of a man who fell into the hands of robbers who took everything the man had, beat him and left him for dead. Two men, a religious man who was a priest and an expert in the law, a Levite, did nothing to help the man. But a Samaritan, a man whom the priest and the Levite looked on with disdain, was the one who bandaged the man's wounds, took him to an inn and took care of him. It was the Samaritan who took out two silver coins and gave them to the innkeeper to look after the injured man. Larry did not have to do what he did when he chose to help me. I knew without a doubt that God placed him in my life at this time to provide a way for me.

The next week, my son arrived back in the states on a two-week leave from his tour of duty in the Middle East. As soon as I saw him, he hugged me with his great big arms around me—both of us trying not to cry. His eyes betrayed him the moment he saw the bald spots and the wispy strands of hair. Two days into his visit, as we sat on my back patio talking, I asked him if he would use the clippers on my hair. Rejecting my request at first, he tried to excuse himself as unqualified. Sitting beneath the umbrella protecting us from the sun, he acquiesced. Hesitantly, he picked up the clippers and turned them on shaping what was left of my hair into a short, fuzzy Mohawk as our tears turned into laughter.

Kirsty, Bridget and Angie, Aubrey's fiancée took turns flying to Dallas to make sure at least one member of the family was with me during each chemo session. My girls and my girlfriends made sure I was never alone unless I expressly asked to be alone. When my family returned to their homes, friends and neighbors stepped into help. Members of the Welcome Class, my Sunday School class, brought food and stayed with me. Friends from Power of Self, my women's leadership class, painted my bedroom and came to visit. My neighbor Carol and her daughter sat with me and helped dust and clean. And Scott mowed my lawn. Trudy and Jay's son, Ross, helped build the flowerbed I had always dreamed of having. And when a storm blew down my fence, I came home from church one Sunday to find Annie and Walter knee-deep in mud, resetting the fence posts in my backyard.

I never got an invitation to join the company in Redmond. I won't deny it; the rejection stung just a little when I learned the other applicant got the position. But I knew that God had another purpose for my life and had used my journey to Redmond to deliver me from my own self-centered ambitions, to redeem me and transform my life. He used it for good so that I could become the woman I was meant to be and live out His purpose for my life.

The world tends to measure success by one's position or title, the size of one's income and the possessions they own. It tends to measure a woman's beauty by her looks and her hair, the size of her breasts, and what she wears. I had been stripped of everything the world used to measure success and beauty. I knew what the world thought, but for the first time in my life, its measures no longer mattered. The only thing that really mattered was my relationship with my God.

God had given me the freedom to choose which road I would take when I came to that crossroad in my life…to follow the world's ways or to follow His ways. When I chose the road less traveled by, He was there to help me through. He knew my pain and sorrow, and He knew the journey I had to take to bring me to surrender. He knew that learning to trust in Him would be a challenge for me. I had been jobless, breastless and hairless, and God allowed my circumstances so that I could come to know Him on a personal level, not only as my Heavenly father, but as a friend who would never betray me. Against all odds, God healed me. Sick, He healed my body. Bald, He blessed me with boldness. Breastless, He restored my femininity. I was bald, bold and beautiful—more beautiful than I had ever felt in my life.

Are not the angels all ministering spirits sent out in service of God to those who will inherit salvation?

Hebrews 1:14

17

Finding Mercy

Finding Mercy

Plano, Texas
Three Years: 2003-2006

God had been merciful with me, and I couldn't help but think about the woman with the beautiful eyes whose name was Mercy.

Day-after-day, as the dawn of the early morning sun crept through my window, I woke whispering her name. And night-after-night in the silence of my bedroom when the chemo coursing through my veins forbade me sleep, I lay in my bed, gazing through the arched transom of my window at the stars and the moon and the very thought of God's healing miracle stole my breath away.

For three years I thought about Mercy and those moments when I sat in the lab of the hospital and watched her do her job. And I wondered who she was.

As though it was yesterday, I remembered the gentleness of her touch as she tied the tourniquet on my arm and gently massaged my vein. It was then, as she drew blood from my already bruised arm that I looked up and saw her eyes for the first time. Something about her eyes seemed to bring peace to my struggling mind and comfort to my grieving heart. Her eyes were unlike anything I ever remembered seeing. They had a quality and depth about them that spoke of kindness and caring, and in my memory of her, her eyes were like liquid pools of compassion. As strange as it sounds—perhaps embarrassed by my own lack or courtesy—I experienced an overwhelming sense of my own imperfection and inadequacy. Aware of my feelings, a sense of unworthiness, I lowered my eyes too embarrassed to look up again.

The moment seemed surreal, as though there was something very different about this woman called Mercy. Only when she turned and walked across the room did I dare to raise my eyes to look at her again. Looking at her from a distance, there was nothing special about her. She seemed unassuming and understated. The maroon of her scrubs matched the colored vials of my blood that she held securely between her thumb and forefinger. And I watched as she rocked the vials back and forth and placed them in a container one-by-one, hoping on the chance that she might turn and look my way so I might see her eyes again.

As much as I tried to quell my desire to know more about her, my curiosity could not be stilled. I could not forget her. I wanted to know who she was…if she was real…if she even existed. As the years passed, my body healed and my strength returned, and my desire to find Mercy grew. Each year when I returned to MD Anderson for my annual checkup, I inquired about Mercy. But her name didn't appear on the database that we looked at, and each time I inquired no one seemed to know who she might be.

I even dared to wonder if she was real or a figment of my imagination—that maybe, just maybe, she was an angel, but my upbringing and education, as conservative as they were, were stumbling blocks for me. In the beginning, more afraid of the criticism and the opinions of others, I rarely spoke about the miracle and secreted both the miracle and my thoughts about Mercy in my heart. Still in awe, I wondered in the quiet moments if she was real or a figment of my imagination.

Over the course of three years and many inquiries, I had almost given up any hope of finding Mercy. Then during a chance meeting with a phlebotomist who worked in a different building across the street from the hospital and the lab where I first met Mercy, I met a woman who knew of someone with the same name. The woman telephoned the Mercy she knew and arranged for me to meet her. Crossing Holcombe Boulevard, I hurried into the hospital and through a labyrinth of now familiar hallways until I found the room I was looking for.

Expectantly, I stepped into the doorway of the lab. My presence seemed to cause a stir, and two women in lab coats bustled forward to inquire about my purpose. Not wanting to cause undo concern for the two women or patients sitting in chairs that lined the walls of the laboratory, I said as quietly as I could, "I'm looking for Mercy."

The shorter of the two women replied, "I'm Mercy." Looking at the woman who spoke, I felt more confused than ever. In my mind's eye, the woman I remembered was taller and much younger than the woman I had met three years before. Questioning myself and all that I had remembered,

I hesitated and wondered if I should continue. Quickly concluding that it didn't matter whether she was the same Mercy I had met years before, I told her the story about God's healing miracle: the pennies, the rainbow and His mercy. It was clear; she had no memory of me. As I finished, the woman searched my eyes considering the implications of what she had heard. Moments later, the woman called Mercy spoke and told me she prayed each morning to be a blessing to someone. I smiled at her words. I knew better than anyone that her prayers to be a blessing had been heard.

I drove home that afternoon questioning whether or not the woman I spoke to that afternoon was the same Mercy that I had met three years before. But in the scheme of things, I knew it really didn't matter. All that mattered was that God used a woman named Mercy whose name and gentleness was what I needed most at that moment in time.

It was clear to me that God in His sovereignty had placed in my path a woman called Mercy who woke each morning with a prayer on her on her lips, "Let me be a blessing to someone today." There was not a single doubt in my mind. I knew that God placed in my path an ordinary woman named Mercy to remind me of His grace and His mercy, so that I could share the story of His miracle and the depth of His love and compassion for you as well.

It was God who allowed me to find two pennies, put them in my shoes and discover the true value of their worth— In God We Trust. It was God who had made a covenant with his people in the time of Noah and the flood and sealed it with a rainbow at the end of the storm. And it was God who used a woman named Mercy, whose eyes were the essence of compassion to show me the depth of his love for me.

The lessons I learned from the pennies, the rainbow and Mercy, I pass on to you. Whenever you see a penny, pick it up. Look at it. Read it. And remember the words inscribed on it—In God We Trust. When you see a rainbow, enjoy its splendor and remember that God keeps His promises. God is faithful through life's storms and can give you strength and peace in the midst of the most difficult time. God understands your situation and is full of mercy and compassion for you.

God can place friends at your side, take you out of a job and still provide for your needs. He can heal old wounds, a wounded spirit, your mind, and your body. Skeptics ask, "Why does God allow bad things to happen? Why does he not perform miracles more often? Why didn't He answer my prayer?" I don't know the answer to those questions.

What I do believe is that miracles are not a reward for anything we do or say. I believe that miracles are a rare form of God's grace, and I believe God uses miracles to let us know that He is all powerful and can do anything He chooses. I believe he uses miracles to confirm who He is and to validate His authority over all things physical and spiritual. And I believe He uses miracles to leave us in awe and wonder so that we will give praise and glory to Him alone.

No one is immune to difficulties; no one is immune to death. Each of us will die—some of us earlier and some of us later. Nothing I have ever done or will do earned me God's favor. On the shores of Lake Washington in the quiet moment of the setting of the sun, with only God at my side, I surrendered my life to Christ, and God had mercy on me a sinner. Unworthy and broken, He restored my feminine spirit so that I could tell others how He change my life so that you might look at your own heart and allow God to transform your life too. God is in control. He is sovereign! He alone can do what no man can do...against all odds.

> *Surely goodness and mercy will follow me*
> *all the days of my life, and I will dwell*
> *in the house of the Lord forever.*
>
> *Psalms 23:6*

He put a new song in my mouth.
A hymn of praise to our God.
Many will see and fear
And put their trust in the Lord.

Psalm 40:3

Epilogue

Epilogue

MD Anderson Cancer Center Houston, Texas
November 17, 2009

When I first started to write the story about God's miracle in the winter of 2004, I ran into a major obstacle. The medication the doctors recommended that I take over a period of five years to reduce the risk of the breast cancer returning made me severely ill. Within days of my first dose of medicine, the joint pain and muscle ache became increasingly unbearable; within weeks, the pain was intolerable. My sister Lynne and my friends, Jenise and Shelley did fine on their post-chemo medication, but I did not. Sharing my symptoms with my oncologist, he reluctantly came to the conclusion that the medicine might be doing more harm than good. With other treatment options exhausted, I made the risky and difficult decision to discontinue taking the medication.

In the meantime, the lymphedema in my left arm progressively worsened and required that I wear a latex sleeve and glove and go to therapy to control the swelling. I continued to try to write, but gave up when carpel tunnel syndrome in my right wrist developed and made typing impossible. Disillusioned, I put the idea of writing the story on the shelf and concentrated on healing.

By the spring of 2004, my straight hair grew back in deep brown curls revealing that fact that Ms Clairol's secret was out, and she wasn't the only one who knew for sure the real color of my hair. Disposing of my wig, I headed for the hairdresser's and had what little hair I had frosted and styled in a cute pixie-like cut just in time for Aubrey and Angie's wedding. Slipping into that perfectly-fitted strapless dress I had dreamed about, I stood on the sandy beach overlooking Chesapeake Bay as my son and his bride exchanged their vows. That evening as the unmistakable voice of Satchmo singing "What a Wonderful World," drifted across the reception hall, my son took my hand and my first prayer, the prayer to dance at my son's wedding, was answered.

That fall, Kirsty and Warren moved back to Dallas from San Francisco and announced that Kirsty was expecting their first child. The following month, Aubrey and Angie called to tell us that Angie was expecting their first child.

Kirsty and Warren's little girl, Sasha Isabella was born on April 7, 2005. That unforgettable day, Kirsty called me to her bedside at the birthing center and whispered with tears of joy glistening in her big brown eyes, "Mom, do you want to hold her?" I held out my arms as my daughter placed her newborn daughter, my first grandchild, in my arms.

Barely two months later, on June 9, 2005, I sat with Angie's parents in the waiting room of the maternity wing in St. Francis Hospital in Richmond, Virginia. Looking out the window as thick, low hanging clouds hovering in the night sky suddenly parted revealing a stunning view of a full moon, the doors to the maternity ward suddenly burst open. Bounding into the room, ecstatic with uncontrollable joy, my son jumped three feet into the air like a running back making the winning touchdown and announced to the world that Zayley Kaye was born.

On February 22, 2008, Angie gave birth to Sydney Evelyn, Zayley's little sister. Eight months later on October 10, 2008, Kirsty gave birth to Niko Owen, Sasha's little brother. I have held four grandchildren in my arms in three years. For the woman who grieved that she would never hold grandchildren in her arms, God's four little gifts in three years was the greatest blessing of all.

With the treatments behind me, I started working for Susan G. Komen for the Cure in 2005. The organization's mission, finding a cure for breast cancer, was dear to my heart, something I believed in. I wanted to spend the rest of my career working for the organization, but a year later, a new CEO came onboard. Over the course of the next six months, the organization went through several rounds of layoffs. Over half of the corporate staff was let go, and I joined the ranks of the unemployed once again. I didn't understand it then, and I don't understand it now, but as much as I loved doing what I was doing, I had to let go. I knew from my past experience, if I waited long enough, I would understand how God would use it for His good.

I knew from the beginning that God had given me the miracle to be a blessing, not just for my family and me, but for others; however, I have to be honest…unemployed and concerned about how I was going to make a living and survive, I couldn't get my arms or my head around how God could do that.

Amazingly, in early December 2006, I received two job offers on the same day...within the same hour...from two different companies. Both were great jobs and both offered excellent benefits and a lucrative salaries. When the offers came in less than an hour apart, I wasn't sure what to do. Analyzing my options, I chose to accept the offer from the company that offered me a signing bonus and was located only a couple miles from my home. Barely four weeks after joining the company, I learned that my position was going to change and the department I worked for was being reorganized.

What had seemed like a dream job turned into a dismal disappointment...almost from the day I joined. I couldn't understand why God, the same God who had given me a miracle, had not protected me. As much as I wanted to point fingers at everyone else, I knew the truth: I had chosen the local job for self-serving reasons—convenience, money and position. The old me had resurfaced quicker than a rocket launch. The truth was, both jobs offered the prestige that I longed for. It really didn't matter which I had taken, in one way or another, the results would have been the same. God had his plans in place for me; and at the time, his plans did not include my working in the corporate world.

Unemployed again, I reopened my former consulting practice to bring in income while I continued to look for full-time work. In the meantime, Angie, my daughter-in-law called to see if I could come and help her out with Zayley and Sydney. The girls were barely a year apart, and Sydney had been born only five days before Aubrey was deployed overseas for his second tour of duty in the Middle East. Angie had done a great job managing on her own while Aubrey was overseas, but after eleven months of being a full-time, single mother to a toddler and an infant, she was exhausted. For the first time that I could remember, I had the freedom to fly to Georgia and help out.

My flight to Augusta required a layover at the airport in Atlanta. That's where I met Jennifer Brown. Waiting for our connecting flights, I shared the story of God's miracle not knowing that Jennifer was looking for a keynote speaker for her church's Good Friday breakfast. A couple weeks later, without ever hearing me speak in public, Jennifer, sure that our meeting was God sent, invited me to her church in Pennsylvania to share my testimony with 300 women at their yearly Good Friday breakfast.

Preparing for the speaking engagement, I read the words of Jesus as he spoke to his disciples about his impending death in John 16:20: "I tell you the truth, you will weep and mourn while the world rejoices. You will grieve, but your grief will turn to joy." The scripture was a perfect fit for the message Jennifer wanted the women to hear. We agreed that the title of the keynote would be: *Your Grief Will Turn to Joy.* God blessed the message that morning, and I returned to Pennsylvania the next weekend to present a two-day program I had designed and developed for women called *Diamonds are a Girl's Best Friend.*

God, all knowing had done it again. He had placed Jennifer, a perfect stranger, in my path to do what He called me to do…to teach, to tell the story of the miracle and to help women rediscover their feminine hearts.

That year I made a penny necklace. It was a treasured reminder of my faith and trust in God. When I wore it, the penny on the necklace captured people's curiosity, and without fail, those who saw it asked me about it. Each inquiry gave me an opportunity to tell the story about God's miracle and make it clear that I wore the penny, not for good luck, but because of the words engraved on it—In God We Trust.

One day, Linda, one of the women who worked at Curves, the place where I went to exercise, introduced me to Marjorie who shared with me her sister's ongoing battle with ovarian cancer. Knowing the story of the miracle behind the penny necklace I wore, Marjorie asked if I would make six necklaces for her. She wanted to give them to her sisters and nieces at their family reunion in the spring as a reminder of their faith and trust in God.

Months later, a friend of Marjorie's sister who lived in Minnesota called and ordered three necklaces. Thrilled that the word was getting out, I made each new necklace and placed it in a card that I had designed that told the story of God's miracle and explained that I wore the necklace as a statement of my faith. More orders came in from people who had heard me speak in Pennsylvania, Virginia and other parts of Texas. Still unemployed, I continued to wonder, "How was I going to earn a living? What did God want me to do?" Day after day, I prayed and ask God to show me where He wanted me to be and what He wanted me to do.

In the spring of 2009, the garden I had always dreamed of having was in full bloom. Bright yellow daffodils that Bridget had given me popped through the freshly turned beds beneath the snow white blossoms of the pear tree. A swing for my grandchildren to play on hung from the lowest limb of the maple tree beside my patio. Red roses cut from the rose bush that Kirsty and Warren had given me for Mother's day decorated my coffee table, and Aubrey was home safe and sound with Angie and the girls.

That August, still working on the book and looking for a job in the middle of a stymied economy, I received a call from a friend of my daughter-in-law who invited me to work at a furniture store in Pilot Point, Texas. The job was good for me, and I quickly discovered that I was happier working in the furniture store than I had been in all the years I had worked in the corporate arena. Working beside Paula and Jacki, my manager and coworker, work was fun. Together, we were a well-matched team as we reset the store and brought out the best in one another. Day after day, in a supportive environment, among co-workers who were genuine and trustworthy, my confidence grew.

Invariably, one of our customers would want to know why I wore a penny necklace. When they asked, I told them. One day, I gathered enough nerve to tell Paula and Jacki about the manuscript that I had been working on. Stepping out on a limb, while the book was still in draft form, I asked if they would consider reviewing the rough manuscript. Finishing the last page, they encouraged me to continue and get the book published.

Buoyed by their encouragement, I drove home from Pilot Point that evening reflecting on the words that Melanie had given me on that small strip of paper six years before, "For I know the plans I have for you, " declares the Lord, "Plans to prosper you and not to harm you, plans to give you hope and a future." Those words had given me hope when there was little to be hopeful about, but the words in the next two verses were the words that showed me what I needed to do...to continue to pray and ask for help.

> *Then you will call upon me and come and pray to me, and I will listen to you. You will seek me and find me when you seek me with all your heart. I will be found by you," declares the Lord, "and will bring you back from captivity."*

When I was laid off, I had known instinctively that the layoff was about God and me. Unlike the people in the story of Jeremiah who were taken captive by the King of Babylon and enslaved in a country far away, I had slipped willingly into work, a different form of captivity that over time became a safe place for me...a place to hide from my own fears and emotions. In the process I became enslaved to a world that measured success based upon achievement, what I did and what I possessed and being me was never good enough. Never being able to have enough knowledge, prestige, wealth and beauty undermined my self-esteem while putting all my efforts into achieving unreachable goals kept me busy all the time. And like a reluctant Jonah swallowed by a big fish, my fear kept me in hiding while my determination to do things my way wreaked havoc in my relationship with God.

Learning that I was going to die was the turning point in my life. When I was fenced in and there was nothing I could do to change my circumstances, God was there. Surrendering my life to God was about learning to trust in Him in everything and for everything. Trust was about surrendering my goals and dreams to allow Him to do what he wanted to do with me... according to His purpose... according to His will.

I began praying and studying scripture to find the answers to my questions. Studying the gospel of Mark, I read the story of the poor widow in chapter 12:42 who gave more than all the rest when she gave two copper coins worth less than a penny, and I thought about the two pennies that I had placed in my shoes that carried the words, In God We Trust and the necklaces I made for others to wear as a statement of their faith.

The question was, "Did I really trust in God for every provision? Was The Copper Coin just wishful thinking on my part or the real thing? Still unemployed that answer seemed clearer. I knew it was time to let go and allow God to use the drive, the talent and the skills He gave me to start a business that glorified Him and honored the story of the miracle He had given me.

As I write the epilogue, God continues to amaze me. One evening as I sat at the dining room table of a friend who had been called to enter into the mission field and go to Chile, we talked about our faith. Suddenly Roberta looked up from her dessert and exclaimed with a sparkle in her eyes, "Isn't God amazing!" Ignited by her thoughts, she asked, "Did you ever consider that God's plans for you were already in place when a little baby was born to a mother who would call her daughter, Mercy? Isn't it amazing that same little girl would grow up and God would place her in the same hospital, in that very room at the very same time that you walked into that lab to have blood work done! What are the odds of that happening?" Roberta's insight was right on target; without God's involvement, the odds of that happening were slim to none.

Looking back over the years since God first placed Mercy in my path, I have learned that God's ways are not our ways, and however much control we think we have over our lives and this universe, ultimately God is in control. He is sovereign.

That Saturday in August 2003 as I stood on the shores of Lake Washington, when all hope was lost, I surrendered my life to God and chose to walk a road less traveled. Laying my burdens at the foot of the cross, I recommitted my life to God and promised to serve Him the rest of my life. I will never understand why God chose to give me a miracle. What I do know is that I have one purpose in my life and that is to glorify God and plant seeds of encouragement and hope by telling you about His miracle; the two pennies, the rainbow and the woman named Mercy, and how He used my circumstances to restore my feminine heart, heal my body, transform my life.

Each time someone orders a piece of jewelry, God God opens the door for them to share their faith with me and me to share my faith with them. Their life stories affirm that making penny necklaces is just one of the things that God has called me to do so that others like me have a simple way to share our faith.

Every piece of jewelry The Copper Coin sells comes with a tiny silver tag. On one side of the tag are the words —*The Copper Coin* reminding me of the faith of the widow who gave more than all the rest. On the other side of the tag are the words—*In God We Trust.*

On November 17, 2009, I returned to MD Anderson for my yearly checkup. Fittingly Harriet was with me when Dr. Abbruzzese walked in to tell me that I didn't need to return for another two years. I had passed my final milestone by a year; I was not five years out, but six years out of treatment and cancer-free. Pulling out the prototype for the cover of the book, *Against All Odds: Two Pennies, A Rainbow and a Woman called Mercy,* to show Dr. Abbruzzese and his PA, Alicia, Dr Abbruzzese gave me an approving nod and acknowledged how hard it was to write a book. When Dr. Abbruzzese left, Alicia smiled and said, "It's so rare that we get these kinds of stories in this office." She was right. I knew all too well that the messenger's job was not easy, and they needed to hear the stories of God's miracles as much as their patients.

Before I left the office, Alicia asked if I would mind stopping on second floor for ten minutes to get my blood drawn. I agreed. Harriet and I left the office and headed straight for the lab.

Waiting for the phlebotomist to read my orders and draw my blood, I thought about how far I had come since 2003. And I wondered what had become of Mercy. I had seen her twice in my life. Once during my first visit in 2003 and another time in 2006, three years before. Sitting quietly, I reminisced. I remembered the first time I saw her as if it were the day before. I remembered the maroon of her scrubs that matched the colored vials of my blood that she had held in her hand. And I remembered watching her as she gently rocked each vial of blood back and forth and placed them one by one in the container in front of her. But the thing that most impacted me was the memory of looking in her eyes. At the time, I couldn't have told you their color without destroying their substance; I could not have described their shape without diminishing their expression. Her eyes were beautiful…so remarkably stunning that my only description for them were liquid pools of compassion.

Sitting there in the phlebotomist cubicle, I looked around at other patients, I was well aware that others in the room were already in the middle of their journey with cancer or just beginning it and would be back many times. As for me, I was happy to know that God willing, I would not be returning for another two years.

The woman who prepared to take my blood politely interrupted my thoughts; she was being called away to help with another patient. Another woman stepped in the cubicle to take her place. It was Mercy.

God took me full circle—back into the loving care of a woman called Mercy so I could thank her and the other women who worked in the lab for the work they do and encourage them through the story of the miracle that God authored; the story of two pennies, a rainbow, and a woman called Mercy... the triumphant story of redemption and grace... a story of God's love and mercy.

> *Surely goodness and mercy will follow*
> *me all the days of my life, and I will*
> *dwell in the house of the Lord forever.*

Psalm 23:6

A Psalm of David

The Lord is my shepherd; I shall not want. He makes me lie down in green pastures, he leads me beside still waters, he restores my soul. He guides me in paths of righteousness for his name's sake. Even though I walk through the valley of the shadow of death, I will fear no evil, for you are with me; You prepare a table before me in the presence of my enemies. You anoint my head with oil; my cup overflows. Surely goodness and mercy will follow me all the days of my life, and I will dwell in the house of the Lord forever.

Psalm 23

Notes

The Lord your God is with you, He is mighty to save.
He will take great delight in you, He will quiet you with his
love, He will rejoice over you with singing.

Zephaniah 3:17

God is not the author of confusion, but of peace.

1 Corinthians 14:33

Notes

The Lord does not see as man sees; for a man looks at the outward appearance, but the Lord looks at the heart.

1 Samuel 16:7

*Don't worry about anything; instead pray about everything; tell God
your needs and don't forget to thank him for his answers. If you do this,
you will experience God's peace, which is far more wonderful than the
human mind can understand. His peace will keep your thoughts and
your hearts quiet and at rest as you trust in Christ Jesus.*

Philippians 4:6-7

Notes

I Love the Lord, for he heard my voice: He heard my cry for mercy. Because he turned his ear to me, I will call on him as long as I live.

Psalm 116:1-2

I lift up my eyes to the hills- where does my help come from? My help comes from the Lord, the maker of heaven and earth.

Psalm 122

Notes

How can I repay the Lord for all His goodness to me?
I will lift up the cup of salvation and call on the name of
the Lord I will fulfill my vows to the Lord in the presence of
all His people.

Psalm 116:12-14

Let everything that has breath praise the Lord.
Praise the Lord.

Psalm 150:6

CPSIA information can be obtained
at www.ICGtesting.com
Printed in the USA
FFOW05n1318151015